Jewellery Making

Jewellery
Making

Emma Gale and Ann Little

To Craig and Davie
For Elspeth Little

With special thanks to John Gale
for his encouragement and enthusiasm
whilst writing this book.

For UK order enquiries: please contact Bookpoint Ltd.,
130 Milton Park, Abingdon, Oxon OX14 4SB.
Telephone: +44 (0) 1235 827720. Fax: +44 (0) 1235 400454.
Lines are open 09.00–18.00, Monday to Saturday,
with a 24-hour message answering service.
You can also order through our website
www.teachyourself.co.uk

For USA order enquiries: please contact
McGraw-Hill Customer Services, PO Box 545, Blacklick,
OH 43004-0545, USA.
Telephone: 1-800-722-4726. Fax: 1-614-755-5645.

For Canada order enquiries: please contact
McGraw-Hill Ryerson Ltd., 300 Water St, Whitby,
Ontario L1N 9B6, Canada.
Telephone: 905 430 5000. Fax: 905 430 5020.

Long renowned as the authoritative source for self-guided learning –
with more than 30 million copies sold worldwide – the *Teach Yourself*
series includes over 300 titles in the fields of languages, crafts,
hobbies, business, computing and education.

British Library Cataloguing in Publication Data
A catalogue record for this title is available from The British Library

Library of Congress Catalog Card Number: On file

First published in UK 2000 by Hodder Headline Ltd.,
338 Euston Road, London, NW1 3BH.

First published in US 2000 by Contemporary Books,
a Division of The McGraw-Hill Companies,
1 Prudential Plaza, 130 East Randolph Street,
Chicago, IL 60601 USA.

The 'Teach Yourself' name is a registered trade mark of Hodder &
Stoughton Ltd.

Typeset by Dorchester Typesetting Group Ltd.
Printed in Dubai for Hodder & Stoughton Educational,
a division of Hodder Headline Ltd., 338 Euston Road,
London NW1 3BH.

Impression number   10 9 8 7 6 5 4 3
Year   2009 2008 2007 2006 2005 2004

Contents

Foreword

Emma Gale and Ann Little are independent jewellers. They are based in workshops in Edinburgh and Dunfermline in Scotland. Graduating in 1995 with 1st-class honours degrees in jewellery from Edinburgh College of Art, under the tuition of Dorothy Hogg, they both received Start Up Awards from the Scottish Arts Council to help them in their first years of business. They are now also teaching part-time in this specialized subject. Their work can be seen in galleries throughout Britain and internationally in temporary exhibitions and permanent collections.

Disclaimer
The authors have highlighted the necessary safety practices for jewellery making throughout this book – no responsibility can be taken for misuse of equipment or materials or for not following the guidelines given. If in doubt the reader should consult their local supplier or tutor for advice.

■ Opposite page: these necklaces are made from nighlight-holders, Volvic bottles and typewriter tape.

Introduction

This book offers a complete course in basic jewellery making to the beginner.

Jewellery making is unique because, unlike other crafts, it uses a variety of different materials. Jewellery encompasses a diverse range of skills and techniques and the exciting results can be worn, adding to its appeal.

Jewellery does not have to be an expensive hobby. Objects such as buttons, threads, paper, natural objects – even toothbrushes – can with a little imagination be used to make sophisticated adornments.

The paper and multimedia section is an introduction to jewellery making and there is no need to invest in specialized equipment for these. The book also shows you how to put together a basic tool kit and work with metal, plastics and resins. If inspired, there are more advanced techniques to learn and advice on setting up a small workshop. Readers may choose to dip into the book at any chapter to concentrate on the aspects that interest them, referring to other sections if necessary.

Although this book is an introduction to the many techniques used in jewellery making, some advanced techniques, such as stone setting, can be explored in more depth by further reading. Before purchasing expensive tools and equipment, attending an evening class at a further education college in your area may result in the confidence to set up a workshop in your own home.

Design inspirations

D esign is the first consideration when creating a piece of jewellery. Insignificant materials such as plastic bottles, night-light holders or typewriter tape can be transformed into desirable jewellery if good design and imagination have been applied. See colour photograph on page 1.

Inspiration for a design can come from a variety of sources. To start with look carefully at your surroundings, for example at buildings, nature, people and animals. Museums are full of ancient and contemporary artefacts. Think about what they are made of, how they have been constructed, where they are from and their surface appearance. Try to distinguish what you like and dislike about these objects. It will soon become obvious what excites and interests you: texture, movement, colour or form. What inspires individuals is a very personal thing, and from the same source material different people will almost always produce completely different designs. Elements from different sources can be combined into one piece of jewellery. It is a good idea to keep a sketchbook of drawings, photographs, postcards, images, textures, ideas and samples for reference.

First of all, consider where on the body the jewellery will be worn. Is it a pair of earrings, a brooch or a necklace, for example? Who will wear it? When will they wear it? If it is for someone you know it can be specifically designed for them. The piece may be subtle, or eye-catching and flamboyant.

Many jewellers are inspired by the material they work with. Instead of designing on paper, unexpected results from experiments can be developed into a final piece. When working with certain materials there are limitations, for example plastic, stone and titanium cannot be soldered so this must be taken into consideration when designing. However, when methods other than soldering are used to attach findings or to join parts together, these can become an integral part of the design.

■ Left: inspiration for a jewellery design can come from many sources.

2

The basic tool kit

S imple jewellery can be made using very little equipment. As you
become more involved in jewellery making you can purchase
more tools as required. The very basics are a jeweller's piercing saw,
a hammer, a file and some pliers.

The full list of basic tools you may find useful while using this book is:

1 saw and range of saw blades

2 pliers: round; ring; flat

3 pliers: parallel

4 files: half-round medium-cut 6-inch file

5 range of needle files

6 snips

7 planishing hammer

8 mallet

9 scribe

10 centre punch

11 poker

12 steel rule

13 ring triblet

14 brass brush

15 burnisher

16 scraper

17 chasing hammer

18 archimedian drill

19 ring stick

20 dividers

Other useful tools not pictured:

emery and wet and dry papers

wire-cutters

hand-held drill and range of drill bits

pin vice

small steel block

vice

For soldering:

21 tweezers: reverse action

22 tweezers: standard

23 binding wire

flux

solders

soldering block

powdered rouge

pickle

soldering torch

Useful equipment you might already have:

Masking tape, small paint brush, permanent marker, pencil, old toothbrush, Blu-Tack, scissors, Plasticine.

■ Left: making jewellery requires some basic tools.   ■ Right: grass necklace by Jennifer Goudie.

Multimedia

Combining different materials together to make jewellery can be very exciting and innovative. Jewellers over the years have incorporated various mixed materials and techniques, moving away from jewellery made predominantly out of metal. Using non-precious materials to make jewellery is an excellent way of being experimental and enjoying yourself.

Materials such as paper, plastic, thread, photographs, stamps, natural dried seed pods, pebbles, plastic bottles and buttons can all become a starting point for jewellery making. The materials might not be precious, but with a little imagination and patience, you can create something with precious qualities. See colour photograph of Grainne Morton's work opposite.

Start to become aware of the objects around you, whether they are man-made or natural. Visit car-boot sales, flea markets or beaches to find inspiration. Even the packaging from food items or magazine cut-outs can be great for jewellery making.

■ Left: mixed media brooch incorporating found objects.

■ Right: grass brooch.

Within this chapter, the tools and equipment are kept to a minimum, and materials are either inexpensive or free. The ideas for making jewellery can all be developed in the home, and are therefore accessible to everyone. Safety aspects are always something to be aware of, especially when using a sharp craft knife, glue or electrical equipment. These items are also kept to a minimum and will be pointed out when they occur through the step-by-step instructions.

Paper

We handle paper every day, probably even without thinking. It is an integral part of money, newspapers, magazines, letters and telephone directories. Paper is around us in such great quantities that we are liable to forget its origins and the extensive amount of work required to make it into the things which we use every day.

For the artist, paper is essential for drawing and design. Materials such as paint, ink, pastels, coloured pencils and charcoal can be used to create patterns and textures. Painting and collage work can both be sources of inspiration when designing jewellery from paper.

Paper, depending on the way it has been treated, can become an extremely durable and waterproof material. It also has other qualities that are beneficial to the jewellery designer. It is light, inexpensive, and readily available in a variety of colours, textures and thicknesses. It also comes in various forms, for example tracing, blotting and watercolour paper.

A list of paper suppliers at the back of the book provides a large selection from which to choose. These include papers from around the world in a variety of textures and colours. Some papers are also available in shiny and satin metallic finishes of gold, silver and bronze.

As the world is becoming more ecologically friendly, you may also consider using recycled paper. Make your own paper or use stamps and sections from magazines and newspapers. All of these materials can be made to look precious and desirable.

The material itself can be a source of inspiration. It becomes three-dimensional through layering, folding, bending, scoring and gluing. The basic equipment needed can probably be found in your cupboard at home; these items may include scissors, craft knife, pencils, ruler and some form of paper glue.

The following sections deal with various paper techniques that are useful in the design and construction of your jewellery.

Laminating paper

Lamination is a process of heat-sealing paper between two sheets of film, making it waterproof and durable. The process is quick and easy, so jewellery can be produced in quantity.

This technique allows you to produce a flat sheet of artwork, possibly in the form of pictures from magazines, a drawing for your sketchbook or even a collage of sweet papers or stamps. Do not worry if the size of your design is larger than the brooch or earrings that you want to make, as colour copiers can either reduce or enlarge any flat image to the size you want. The image is then placed between two sheets of clear laminating film and heat-treated to bond the two pieces together. The laminating film is available in a variety of weights and you should use the type that suits your design. For example, if you are laminating thicker card, use thin laminating film because the card will give it strength. Magazine images are produced on fine paper, and therefore a thicker laminating film is required. It is worth bearing in mind that the laminating film will give extra thickness to your design, so take this into account before you start.

Most art colleges and photocopy shops have laminating machines and will be able to supply you with the film. If you do not have access to a laminating machine, used with care a household iron will do the job.

Laminating with a household iron

You will need: collage or images to laminate, e.g. magazines, stamps or sweet papers; laminating paper; household iron; jeweller's burnisher or spoon; firm flat surface; thin paper (tracing or greaseproof); jewellery findings; steel wire; glue; scissors.

1   Place an image between two sheets of laminating film. The sheets should be slightly larger than the actual size of your design.
2   Put the iron on a low setting, for example for silk or polyester. Experiment on samples before you start to work on your final piece. The thickness of your laminating film will determine the heat required.
3   Always iron on a hard flat surface. Make sure that the surface is protected, especially if it is wood as this will burn.
4   Iron the laminate in-between two thin pieces of paper – tracing paper or greaseproof paper – as this protects the laminate from direct heat and also protects the iron from the laminating film.
5   Hold the iron on the laminate for as long as is required. Start with eight to ten seconds, holding for slightly longer if necessary.
6   To make sure your piece is completely sealed, rub over the surface with a jeweller's burnisher or the back of a metal spoon.
7   Always remember not to leave the iron unattended or on top of the laminating film, as it will eventually melt and the paper will burn.
8   Do not turn the iron up. If necessary keep it on a low temperature for a longer length of time.
9   Cut away any excess laminating film, but leave a slight edge of approximately 2 mm as this leaves a good seal.
10 Jewellery findings can be attached with glue. Alternatively, the laminated strip can be punched and the findings attached with leather cord, silk threads or chain. For suppliers of jewellery findings see the back of the book.

An example of this type or work is evident in the jewellery produced by Sue Downing. The images she uses are cut from magazines or collages from her sketchbook. As a starting point Sue will often scour second-hand shops and car-boot sales looking for magazines from the 60s, 70s and 80s. Her inspiration in general comes from sources as diverse as dogs, flowers, cakes, lamps and general household equipment. Often the images that she wants to use are too large to fit into a brooch, so she will reduce them on the photocopier to meet her needs. They are cut out, positioned and laminated, then attached to clothing using a very simple pin made from stainless steel wire or clips. See the photograph below of one of Sue's creations, a tiara.

■ Silver tiara with laminated magazine images and cubic zirconium.

Other methods

Self-adhesive plastic

For an alternative method that produces similar results to iron laminating, try placing an image in-between two sheets of self-adhesive plastic and pressing together. A thicker image may be required using this method to give the required rigidity.

Paper varnish

Using this method, the image has a coat of varnish applied to its surface using a brush. The more coats of varnish applied, the stronger the piece will become. Often, a solvent, such as white spirit or turpentine, will be needed to clean the brush if the varnish is not water-based. The instructions for use will be attached to the bottle. There is usually a required drying time prior to the application of the next coat. It is important to wear a form of mask during this process, as the fumes can become quite potent in an unventilated room.

Layering paper

The layering of paper, when built up, can create a three-dimensional object. Cut-out basic shapes can be strung one after the other, or glued together, to build up a shape. Something as simple as a hole punch can be a great disc-cutting tool.

■ Left: Angela O'Kelly's necklace features layered paper and fabric.

■ Above: paper necklace with drawings and silver, detail.

Making a pair of simple earrings

You will need: paper; hole punch; glue; findings; needle; round pliers; thread or wire; optional beads.

1 A simple pair of earrings can be made by collecting the round paper discs from a hole punch. The paper can be any variety, for example newspaper, metallic or tissue, as long as it fits into the hole punch.

2 The paper can be made waterproof by painting on varnish.

3 Pierce a hole through the centre of each disc using a needle.

4 String the discs onto thread or wire. Use a needle or taper the end of the wire to a point to pierce the discs. Alternatively, glue them together to form one bead.

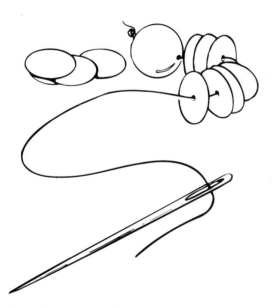

■ Threading the paper discs from a hole punch onto thread

5 The effect can be enhanced by the use of bought beads, for example polystyrene, wooden, plastic or metal, and these can be painted to suit. These can be placed in-between the discs to add interest.

6 Bend up the end of the wire to hold everything in place, or alternatively, if you are using thread, tie a knot in the end and add a blob of glue.

7 Earring hoops or fasteners can then be attached with the thread or wire.

■ Finished earrings attached to earring wires

Emma Gale's paper necklace (see Chapter 10) is made by cutting discs from various Japanese and Indian handmade papers. The round discs were produced with a disc-cutting tool made from steel tubing with a sharpened edge. The tool was made specifically for the design. This allowed many identical discs to be cut out quickly and easily. Perspex and silver discs were cut to the same size as the paper and all strung like beads onto a steel wire.

Rolled paper

Beads can also be constructed by rolling up paper shapes. This technique once again demonstrates how the layering of paper forms a three-dimensional object.

Rolling beads

You will need: paper; scissors; craft knife; paint; ruler; fine rods (knitting needles, pencil, or a cocktail stick); glue; paper varnish; silk thread, cord or wire.

1 First of all choose your paper. The paper can be any variety as long as it rolls up well, so keep to something fairly thin. You may want to paint one side, so your bead is made up of two colours.

2 Draw a template for a triangle and cut it out. It can be made with larger or smaller dimensions depending on the size of bead you want. For example, it you lengthen the triangle this will make a thicker bead.

3 Draw or score round the template to make several triangles and cut them out. A different effect can be achieved by tearing out the triangles along a scored line, making the edge softer and more delicate.

4 Curl the triangle around a fine rod, such as a knitting needle, pencil or cocktail stick. To stop the bead unravelling glue the tips or spread the glue over the whole of one side. If you are using a wooden cocktail stick, make sure it is waxed to stop the glue from sticking.

5 Leave the beads to dry.

6 Once dried, the beads can then be varnished to give a glossy finish, or just kept in their original state.

7 To make a necklace, string the beads onto silk strands, wire or beading thread. Additional beads can also be strung in-between to create a variety of looks. Try making lots of beads for a really long necklace. The ends can be tied and the neckpiece wrapped around the neck several times.

Papier-mâché

Papier-mâché is another simple technique that can be used in jewellery making. There are two methods of producing papier-mâché: either by making a paper pulp or by layering paper. The pulp method involves submerging paper in water until it becomes very mushy and adding wallpaper paste or a mixture of flour and water. The layering method uses torn strips of paper layered on top of one another and bonded together with wallpaper paste. Depending on the object you wish to make, the two different methods can create different effects. The layering method is good for producing hollow, light forms, while the pulp method means you can form solid, denser objects. Ideas can be endless as the technique lends itself to any shape or size. Decoration can be added with paint, stones or natural objects, such as leaves.

Layering technique

This method gives lightweight beads with a smooth finish.

Papier-mâché beads: the layering method

You will need: paper torn into strips; a small object, for example a table-tennis ball; wallpaper paste; PVA glue; bowl or small bucket for mixing paste; petroleum jelly; brush; craft knife; paint; paper varnish; pin vice; small drill bit; cord or wire.

1 Choose your paper. Brown paper or wallpaper lining give good surfaces to paint on later and are also ideal for papier-mâché objects. Tear the paper into small strips.

2 Choose a small object around which you can layer your paper. For example, a table-tennis ball will make a lovely, large, round bead.

3 Make up your wallpaper paste by following the manufacturer's instructions. Start by making a small amount – you can always make more if required.

4 Cover the object in petroleum jelly so that the paper, once dried, will come away with ease.

5 Start to build up the layers by brushing paste on to both sides of each paper strip, and bond them around the object. Use your hands to smooth them together.

6 After about three to four layers, depending on the thickness of the paper used, leave the ball to dry. You can continue adding layers once the ball has dried, if you feel it is not thick enough.

7 Once dried cut round the middle through the layered paper, until you reach the original object, and pull the two halves apart.

8 Put the two halves back together using glue to make a hollow bead. Cover the join with some more strips of paper. These can be bonded with PVA glue and left to dry.

9 The bead is then ready to be painted. Acrylic and gouache paints are good for this. You could even glue on stones, or give your bead a glossy finish using a paper varnish.

10 Using a small drill bit in a pin vice, screw into the papier-mâché bead and make two holes through which the thread can pass.

Pulp

This way of working is a bit like modelling with Plasticine or clay, as the paper needs to be squeezed and shaped. This method is a quicker way of building up than the layering method and different surface textures can be created using finer or thicker pulp.

Making a pulp papier-mâché bead necklace

You will need: paper; bowl or small bucket; old food processor; wallpaper paste; plastic sweet-cutter; petroleum jelly; paint; paper varnish; jump rings; cord or wire.

1 Choose any small plastic sweet-cutter. These are available in lots of shapes, for example hearts, stars, moons, squares, triangles. Place the cutter on a non-stick board. Cover the inside of the shape with petroleum jelly to stop any sticking.

2 Choose your paper – brown paper or wallpaper lining are good – and tear it up into a bowl of hot water, leaving it to soak.

3 Put the soaked paper with the water through an old food processor or blender until it becomes mushy. Alternatively, rub the mixture through your fingers until the paper has broken up.

4 Strain off the excess water from the pulp, and place in a bowl or small bucket. Then add the wallpaper paste, following the manufacturer's instructions.

5 Squeeze and knead the paste in with the pulp, making sure it does not become too thick. Remember the mixture has to be malleable.

6 Push the pulp mixture into the shape with your fingers or a small spoon. Make sure you fill all the corners and the shape is completely compact.

7 Let the bead dry – somewhere warm like an airing cupboard is ideal.

8 Once dry, ease out your papier-mâché shape and paint it.

9 Varnish your bead with a paper varnish to give extra strength and a glossy finish. The addition of small colourful stones could also be interesting.

10 A small jump ring can then be attached with wire so you are able to hang your bead from a necklace or leather thong to make a simple pendant.

Other paper techniques to try

There are many other ways of making decorative marks and creating form in paper; experimentation is the best way to discover these. Try folding the paper in various ways, for example by using the Japanese art of paper folding called origami. There is no cutting or gluing involved – just folding. Coloured pieces of special origami paper already cut to size can be purchased from art and craft shops so all you have to do is fold. It is a wonderful way of producing a three-dimensional object that is delicate and light. Other ideas to try are: fluting the paper, piercing into it, weaving strips together and pressing in objects.

■ This shoulderpiece made from paper and wire is inspired by the feathers on a bird.

Textile ideas

There are many textile techniques that can be applied to jewellery making. These include: embroidery (either by hand or machine), appliqué; silk painting; felt-making; knitting; crocheting; weaving; braiding. It is also possible to develop these textile techniques in other media, for example crocheting, knitting and braiding can all be produced using fine metal wire (see Chapter 6). You can decorate and embellish fabric with gold and silver threads, beads, sequins, buttons, ribbons and many other bits and bobs. Ideas again are endless, with materials available at most large department stores and craft suppliers. Specialist fabric and wool shops often have a remnant box where you can rummage to find odds and ends. Second-hand and charity shops are also good places to find materials.

■ Above: this drawing of a bird is one of many that inspired pieces such as the shoulderpiece on the previous page.

Felting

The bracelet made by Emma Gale (see right) is made up from silver Perspex discs, and paper and felt beads. The felt beads are formed from raw sheep fleece, which has been cleaned and treated so it is soft and easy to use. The fleece needs to be pulled apart into small pieces, then washed in hot and soapy water. This is then rolled into a tightly compacted ball of woollen fibres. The heat from the water and friction process causes the fibres to matt together, so forming a felt bead. The fleece can be dyed in its raw state or when made into beads. It is also possible to buy fleece already dyed in small quantities from the specialist suppliers listed at the back of the book. Decoration can be added in the form of paint, small beads, buttons and sequins, or they can be left just plain.

■ Right: bracelet of felt beads, silver, paper, Perspex and gold leaf.

Making felt beads

You will need: fleece (either dyed or natural); bowl; hot soapy water; strong thread; needle; paint, beads, buttons, or sequins (optional).

1 Choose your fleece. This can be purchased, either carded or uncarded and left in its raw state or dyed, from specialist craft suppliers. It is possible to dye your own fleece by using fabric dyes, but at this stage a selection of pre-dyed and carded bags of fleece is ideal.

2 Tear off small sections from the fleece and gently roll them into a loose ball shape. Immerse this in hot soapy water. Kneed and roll the fleece around in the palm of your hand until it starts to matt into a hard ball.

3 Take the ball and place it in a bowl of clean water, squeezing away all the excess soap.

4 This is optional, but placing the balls in a washing machine on a fast spin helps to felt them further and rids the ball of excess water.

5 Place the balls in a dry place, either near a radiator or in an airing cupboard.

6 Once dried the beads can be decorated with paint, tiny glass beads, buttons and sequins, or left plain and strung with strong thread and a large needle into a necklace or bracelet.

Pompoms

With all the wonderful coloured and textured fine wool and metallic silk thread available, the traditional textile technique of pompom making is a fun way to make jewellery. As well as necklaces, bracelets and even a wacky pair of earrings, pompoms can be used to enhance other accessories, such as hats, scarves and clothes in the form of toggles and buttons. The pompom can be as large or as small as you require, and can be trimmed down to any size.

Pompom making

You will need: wool or thread; card; scissors; pair of compasses (or something to draw round).

1 Select your wool or thread. If it comes in a large ball, wrap a smaller amount around an empty cotton reel, or a wine-bottle cork, so it will pass through the middle of your card template easily.
2 To make your card templates (card from a cereal packet is ideal), use a pair of compasses to draw two circles, one inside the other. The size of the template determines the size of the pompom.
3 Cut out two matching templates with a pair of scissors.
4 Place the two pieces of card together. Form a loop with your thread and knot around both pieces of card. Now start wrapping the wool, through the centre, up and over, and round the card in a clockwise direction.

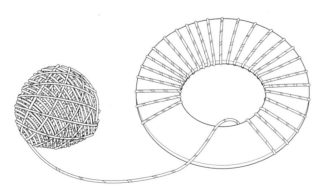

■ Two cut-out templates are placed together and the wool or thread is wrapped around them.

5 Build up the layers until you are left with a small hole in the centre. Tie the loose ends into one of the wrapped threads.
6 Here comes the tricky part! Dig your scissors through the wool and between the two card templates. **Find the middle section between the two pieces of card.** Cut the threads all the way round. Slightly prise apart the two halves of card and bind up the middle tightly with the same thread. Pull away the card.

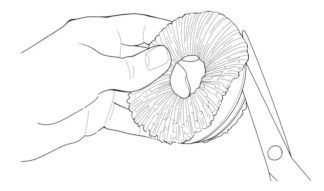

■ When all the wrapping is complete, cut between the two templates with a pair of scissors.

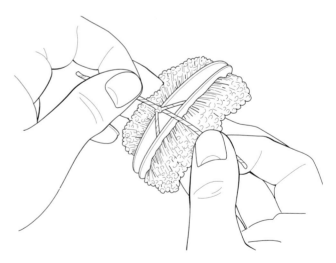

■ Prise apart the templates and tie the middle section to make your pompom.

7 Ruffle up your pompom until it becomes a round ball. Using a pair of sharp scissors, trim down to size.

Now you can go on to produce numerous pompoms, all varying in colour, texture and size. They can be strung together like the felt beads into a wonderful neckpiece or a longer version with larger pompoms would create a fabulous scarf. Elastic threaded through each one means you could make a bracelet, which can be put on and taken off easily. Have fun – the possibilities are endless!

Stringing beads

Stringing beads onto thread is one of the oldest forms of jewellery making. Materials such as plastic, wood, shell, glass, ceramic, as well as found objects, have all been used to make beads that have then been strung onto either thread or wire. Threading can be as conventional or as unconventional as you want, and different coloured threads can be used, with additional knots and sections that dangle if desired. Beads can follow a pattern of small to large with a tiny knot in-between each bead. The knots not only add to the design and flexibility, but also add protection if the string breaks, as only one bead will be lost. It is a good idea to thread with two strings, so that if one thread breaks the other one will support the beads.

Silk thread is extremely strong and is better than cotton, which is more prone to rotting. Silk is available in a range of different thicknesses and colours and is great for knotting. Nylon thread is also very strong, but is not very good for knotting and the ends have to be glued into place. Wire is very strong and can be manipulated to form any shape. Wire is now available that is extremely fine, very strong and covered in a plastic coating, enabling the beads to slip on easily. Chain is also great for hanging beads.

Make sure the thread you are using is fine enough to go through the bead hole. Beads made from stone are usually manufactured so should all have approximately the same sized hole, but some will have been drilled by hand and may vary in size. If you want to knot in-between each bead, the thread has to be at least six times the length of the necklace.

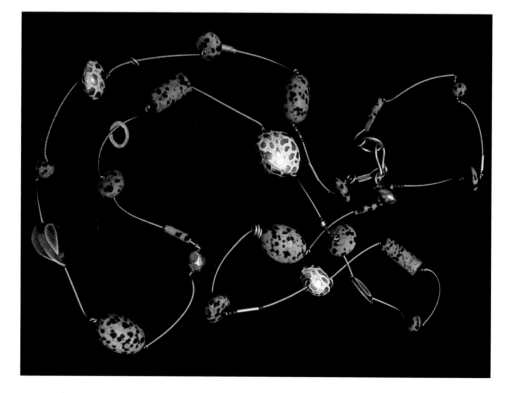

■ Steel wire necklace with Dalmatian jasper and silver etched beads. Notice how the wire has been knotted to keep the beads in place.

The end threads are looped through catch fittings, which can be bought or made (see Chapter 10). The end loops are the most vulnerable so should be surrounded with gimp. This is a spiral of very fine tightly coiled wire with a hole through the middle, like a tube. The gimp fits onto the end sections of thread to add protection and also makes the ends neater. It is possible that even the gimp will eventually wear away over a long period of time, especially as the catch rubs while the piece is being worn. Gimp comes in gold and silver and can be purchased from jewellery suppliers.

Bead threading

You will need: fine steel to make into a threading needle; scissors; beads; clear nail varnish or glue; gimp; silk, nylon thread or threading wire; catch; fine tweezers.

1 Arrange the beads in order for stringing, placing them in the fold of a book or a fold in a piece of paper to stop them from rolling away.

2 Select your thread. If you want to knot in-between each bead, cut a piece six times the length of the necklace.

3 Make a threading needle if there isn't one provided with the thread. To do this, use extremely fine steel wire. Leaving a small hole at one end for the thread to pass through, like a needle, bend the wire in half and twist the two sections together.

4 Thread a piece of gimp through the needle and then thread this through one half of the catch and tie a tight knot. The loose ends can then be glued with either a clear adhesive glue or clear nail varnish. Leave this to dry before starting to thread on the beads.

5 Start to thread on the beads. Either tie a knot in-between each or let them slot against each other. The best way to achieve a tight knot is to tie the thread around a needle in a small pin vice and push it up tightly against the bead. This way the knots will be evenly spaced down the length of the necklace and will keep each bead in place.

6 Finish the end as you did previously, using the gimp, and glue on the tied knot. Double back through the last bead with the small end thread to give a tidy finish.

■ Necklace of rock crystal oval beads, silver and 24-carat yellow roll printed gold.

■ Right: necklace of slate beads inlaid with silver dots and labradorite beads.

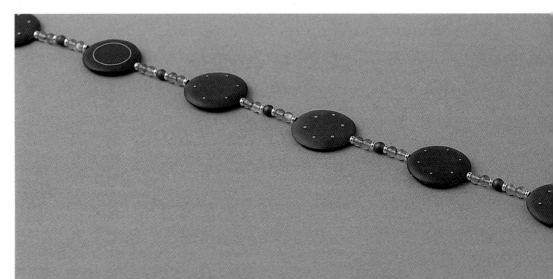

4

Metals

M etals have been used for thousands of years to produce practical and ornamental objects.

Our understanding of metal has been a gradual learning process. Metals present in their pure state, such as gold, were the first to be utilized, then a method of extracting metals from their ores was developed. This technique was called smelting and involved heating the ore to extract metal. Metals in their pure state are very soft and have limited uses but a breakthrough was made with the discovery that combining metals changed their characteristics. This process, called alloying, made it possible to produce stronger and harder metal. Alloying can alter the colour, melting point, hardness and malleability of a metal. Bronze is an alloy of copper and tin.

■ Mixed metal brooch.

Metal elements differ from other elements because of their malleable, ductile and tensile qualities. They are extremely good heat and electricity conductors and can be polished to a shiny surface. The malleability of metal allows it to be stretched in all directions by hammering, rolling, stamping etc. Its ductility makes it possible to draw down wire, stretching it to make it longer and thinner. The tensile strength of metal prevents it from snapping or cracking if it is annealed. Different metals are malleable to different degrees but their workability can be altered by alloying. It is this ability to shape and work metal without it breaking and splitting which is the essence of metalworking.

Annealing

Although metal can be shaped by hammering and bending, after continuous working it will begin to harden and become less malleable. To restore metal to a good working condition, a method called annealing is used. Annealing is the process of heating metal to a certain temperature to relieve the strains created while working. The metal to be annealed should be raised over the fire brick on a stand which allows heat to circulate around the whole piece. The temperature of the piece is judged by the colour of the metal. To see the colour of the metal more easily switch off any lights or work in a dimly lit area. Heat the metal evenly using a blow torch.

Sterling silver and gold should be heated until they glow a dull red, then quenched in water as soon as the red colour disappears. Red gold, copper and brass should be heated until they are a medium red colour, then quenched. Steel has to be heated to a very bright red and then left to cool. It will take practice to identify the subtle colour changes. When annealing long pieces of wire, wrap them into a tight coil and tie together with binding wire. This creates a thick ring, making it easier to heat evenly, and prevents stray thin wires melting.

The annealing process must be repeated whenever the metal becomes work hardened.

Precious metals

Not all metals have commercial uses and even fewer are suitable for jewellery production. The attractive properties of metal which lend themselves to use in jewellery are workability, colour, resistance to tarnish and rarity. They are usually divided into two groups: precious and base metals.

The precious metals – gold, platinum and silver – are popular in jewellery making because they are chemically stable. This means they resist tarnishing and erosion by acids, making them hard-wearing and attractive. They are also relatively scarce which adds to their value.

Platinum

Platinum is the most expensive precious metal. It is also the heaviest, the least reactive, the most rare and the most difficult to work with. It is extremely stable and does not oxidize. Unusually it can be polished, then soldered and when allowed to cool naturally will look as shiny as it did before heat was applied. Because of its very high melting point (almost twice that of silver) it needs intense heat to anneal and solder. All equipment must be kept very clean when working with platinum as contamination by silver, aluminium or iron can cause cracking when it is heated. This is impossible to rectify without cutting out the section and patching. Platinum is usually a metal reserved for the accomplished metalworker, predominantly because of its price and its unusual properties.

Gold

Gold is a lovely material to work with. It is so malleable that it can be hammered into sheet thinner than foil. In its pure form gold is extremely soft. In this soft state it has certain uses, but it is generally alloyed with other metals to make it a more suitable working material. The different colours and carats of gold are produced by alloying. Red gold has a higher percentage of copper, while white gold is produced by adding zinc and nickel. The number of carats in gold refers to the amount of pure gold in an alloy, for example 24-carat gold contains more gold than 9-carat gold. Gold carats should not be confused with the carats associated with stones. They are a measurement of weight, not of quality. Gold is an expensive material to work with. The price of it fluctuates every day. If you want to try working in gold begin by introducing a small amount into a piece you are making in another metal.

■ Right: oxidized silver and gold brooch with drilled holes.

Silver

Silver is a very popular material for jewellery making. In its pure form it is very soft. This fine silver is used for stone setting because it is easy to push over the stone, but generally silver is alloyed. The most common alloy of silver used in jewellery is sterling silver, which is easy to work with and is not as expensive as gold. One problem of working in sterling silver is fire stain.

Fire stain

When silver alloy is heated, the copper it contains reacts with the oxygen in the torch flame, creating dark grey stains of copper oxide under the surface of the silver. These grey patches are unsightly but difficult to avoid. There are special fluxes that can be bought to paint over a whole piece before heating. They work by preventing contact between oxygen and the metal surface but, because they are fluxes, they encourage solder joins to run. The only method to remove fire stain is to patiently polish it out. You can try using emery paper, or a water of ayr stone. It takes time and patience. If there is a lot of fire stain you may have no alternative but to file the whole piece **until the fire stain covers the surface of the metal**. Although this will create a slightly duller surface that may tarnish quickly, it is more satisfactory than patches.

■ Above: 18-carat yellow gold and silver rings.

Base metals

Base metals include copper, nickel, aluminium, zinc and tin and are abundant in comparison to the precious metals. Copper is commonly used for jewellery because it is very malleable and cheap, although it tarnishes easily. Brass is yellow-coloured and is harder than copper. Gilding metal has a similar appearance to copper but is distinguished by the more yellow colour of the cut edge. Another base metal is bronze which is often used for casting jewellery and larger objects such as sculptures.

Aluminium is a cheap lightweight material. An oxide film can be formed on its surface using electricity. This film can then be dyed bright colours and patterned using resists.

The refractory metals

The refractory metals include titanium and niobium. They can have brightly coloured surfaces created using heat or electricity. Although strong and light they are quite difficult to saw, file, hammer and bend and cannot be soldered. Time must be taken at the design stage to work out inventive ways of joining. Riveting, slotting and bending are suitable methods.

Creative jewellers producing one-off pieces do not restrict themselves to one material. Some combine precious metals with non-precious materials, such as paper or plastic. If working on a large scale you may not be able to afford to use expensive materials. Remember to experiment with mixed media. If done sensitively and creatively, the most unlikely combinations of materials can look stunning. Increasingly it is the design and effect of a piece of jewellery which is more important than the value of the material from which it is made.

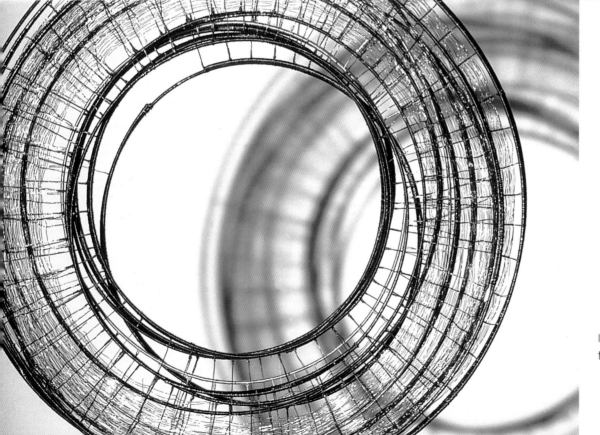

■ Neckpieces made from steel wire.

5

Basic jewellery techniques

There are a few basic techniques which, when followed, will allow you to make most items of jewellery in metal. Saw piercing, drilling and filing are also techniques that can be used on plastics and other materials. Soldering requires more equipment and because of the fumes and heat created, a separate workspace is advisable.

You may wish to develop and experiment with simple methods of joining until you become more confident.

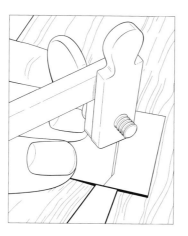

■ Saw piercing a piece of metal on a bench peg.

Saw piercing

Saw piercing is one of the first procedures you need to know when working with metal and is a starting point to many other processes. A detailed design drawn onto a sheet of metal can be pierced out with a jeweller's saw. There are various gauges of blades used depending on the metal thickness.

Saw blade grades finest 6/0, 5/0, 4/0, 3/0, 2/0, 1/0, 0, 1, 2, 3, 4, 5, 6 coarsest.

The finest blades are used on delicate sheet work and the coarser ones are used for thicker metal or other materials such as plastic. Even the thickest saw blade is prone to snapping, so do not worry if your blades keep breaking, it just takes practice – even professional jewellers break saw blades!

To insert the blade into the frame, make sure the teeth are running down towards the handle and in the other direction to the saw frame. You will know if the saw blade is the wrong way up because it will not cut the metal with ease. Tighten one end of the blade into the top end of the saw. Holding on to the handle, push the framework up against the bench and then tighten the bottom screw. Your blade should be taut across the two ends of the framework, and when plucked will sound like a violin.

When sawing into the metal, relax and let the blade do the work; it will cut on the downward motion, so you can form a rhythm while guiding it along. The saw frame should be held in an upright position, otherwise the blade will become stuck and break. To make the initial cut into the metal, hold the flat sheet firmly against the workbench wooden peg (see Chapter 15 for photo of workbench). Put a small file mark at the edge or very gently using your finger at the side of the blade, saw up and down until an initial line has been made. Once you have grasped the art of sawing straight lines, try turning corners. This involves keeping the saw moving on the same spot, but turning the metal at the same time, then when facing in the right direction sawing forward again. Make sure you keep your fingers away from the cutting line. If a saw blade breaks in the metal it can easily be removed by using pliers.

■ Earrings of copper, enamel and brass which demonstrate intricate saw piercing and enamel work.

Drilling

Safety
If using a large free-standing electrical drill, tie back long hair, wear safety goggles and ensure you have a good grip on the piece being drilled. A special drill vice is useful for holding work.

Sometimes a design has an open middle section while the surrounding framework is solid metal. This can be achieved by drilling a small hole in the centre and threading the blade through the hole, **then connecting the saw frame and blade** as usual. To drill a hole in a flat sheet of metal, position a centre punch and hit it with a hammer. The slight indentation in the metal helps the drill locate easily. Drill bits, like saw blades, are available in many different sizes and can be used in a variety of different types of drill. These include hand, bow, archimedean, pin vice and electric drills. Except for the electrical standing drill, all are relatively inexpensive and a drill is a necessary piece of equipment for your tool box.

To drill into a curved surface, slightly flatten out that particular area with a small file so that the drill does not slide off. Rather than marking the spot with a centre punch, as this will cause an unwanted dent, take a scribe or scraper and scratch in a tiny indentation for the drill to locate. Always hold the metal down firmly with your hand or masking tape. Drilling on a block of wood prevents making holes in the workbench.

Small drilled holes can also be used as a method of decoration. Lots of tiny holes drilled closely together, like an old silver tea strainer, can be very effective (see Anna Gordon's brooch on page 21).

Filing

A file is a tool used for the shaping, forming and finishing of metal. Filing is usually the next stage after saw piercing, as the rough edges created by the saw blade need to be smoothed. There are many different files available, each with a specific job. They vary in size, shape and coarseness, and with each group there will be a range of fine, medium and coarse grades. For one particular job you might use between three and four various files before reaching the final finishing stage of emery paper and polishing. Coarser files take away more metal so these are usually used to start with, graduating down to finer ones.

Files grades rough 00, 0, 1, 2, 3, 4, 5, 6 very smooth

File shapes round, half-round, flat, triangular, square, crossing, knife edge.

The hand files used by jewellers range from the smallest, finest files, called escapement files, up to Swiss pattern files available in 6-inch (150mm), 8-inch (200mm) or 10-inch (250mm) lengths. When bought, these larger files do not include a handle, but wooden ones can be purchased separately. There is a technique to fitting a handle securely.

■ Brooch - base metals.

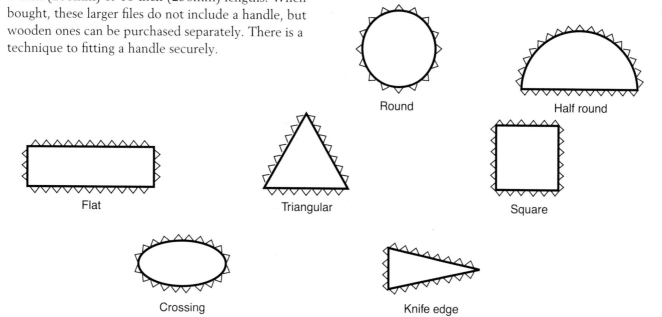

Round

Half round

Flat

Triangular

Square

Crossing

Knife edge

■ Cross section of files.

Fitting a wooden handle to a file

You will need: a basic tool kit; wooden handle.

1 Hold the file vertical with the tang (the pointed end that fits into the handle) sticking upwards and your hands holding the file at the very bottom.
2 Using your torch heat the tang, directing your flame upwards, so preventing the rest of the file from heating up and burning your hand.
3 When the metal tang turns red push it firmly into the wooden handle so the hot metal burns into the wood.
4 If the file requires pushing onto the handle a fraction more, secure it in a vice, protected with a cloth or vice jaw protectors, and tap the end of the wooden handle with a mallet until it feels tight and secure.

All files have been designed so that the teeth cut on the forward stroke. File away from the body, lifting the file a fraction on the upward motion and adding just enough pressure to cut the metal. Try not to force the file against the metal as this could create a buckling edge and also makes a terrible noise! Use the whole length of the file and don't let it drag as this can eventually wear a file down and clog it with metal filings. These filings can be removed with a wire brush. For curved inside shapes, half-round, crossing or round files would be used.

Most jewellery is small enough to be hand held and filed, but larger pieces of work that are awkward to hold can be clamped to a bench or held securely in a vice. Always take care not to mark the work with the teeth on the vice. Use vice protectors or wrap the work in a protective cloth. Remember filing is a method of removing metal, it cannot be replaced, so take care and be patient.

Soldering

Safety
- *Do not touch hot tools or metal after soldering.*
- *Try to avoid breathing in fumes produced during soldering.*
- *Always remember to turn gas appliances off.*
- *Avoid getting pickle on skin or clothing. It burns holes in clothing and should be washed off immediately.*

Soldering is the joining of metal using a special metal alloy, which when heated to a certain temperature creates the join.

Gas torches

Soldering is accomplished using a gas torch. There are a variety of different types, including compressed air torches and bottled gas torches. In a small workshop a bottle gas torch is ideal. The bottle contains either propane or butane gas and has the air compressed inside. They can be purchased from any gas supplier in a variety of sizes, and a small torch can be stored neatly away in a cupboard. Check with your supplier which gas you need to match the type of torch you have and ask them to connect it for you.

■ Purse - Mokume Gane silver and base metals.

Compressed air torches are often used in colleges or large workshops and run from a major gas supply; they are often used for work that requires more heat, such as silversmithing larger pieces. Mouth-blown torches can also be used with bottled gas. The air is supplied by blowing through a tube. Some jewellers find they have more control with this type of torch but it takes practice to be able to use it with skill.

Fluxes

Flux is used with solder to help it flow along a join. Flux is available as a paste, a powder or a liquid. The most commonly used is borax. It is bought as a cone and used in a special ceramic dish. Water is added to the ceramic dish and the cone is rubbed vigorously in the water to form a creamy paste. The paste is then painted onto the join ready to be soldered. This flux can be used for all general purpose solders, but there are fluxes that are used on high-temperature metals, such as gold and platinum. These can be purchased from specialist jewellery suppliers.

Remember that metal surfaces should be free of grease and dirt before using flux. This can be achieved by using a fine-grade emery paper over the two metal surfaces. The flux should only be placed on the area to be soldered and nowhere else, or the solder will run everywhere.

Solders

The solders used in jewellery for brass, copper, silver, gold and platinum are called hard solders. Soft solders derive from alloys of tin and lead and have a very low melting temperature. They do not form a strong bond and the solder join can often be seen even after filing.

Most soldering in jewellery will be done with silver solder, which is used for working with brass, silver and copper. It is made up of a mixture of alloys that include silver itself, copper and zinc. The quantities of these alloys can be altered in the solder to create the different melting temperatures. These are called **hard**, **medium**, **easy** and **extra easy**. Hard solder is used first,

if there are several joins in one piece. The next join is made with medium solder, then followed by easy. These stages allow you to heat the same piece of metal without the last join melting. If your work only needs one soldering, then use a lower melting solder such as medium or easy. Extra easy solder has the lowest melting temperature and can be used for small repair jobs or if all the other solders have already been used on a piece. The silver content in extra easy solder is low, giving it a yellow appearance and making it good for working with brass.

Gold solder

There are also hard, medium and easy gold solders. These are available in different colours and carats of gold. Gold solders are mainly made up of gold, copper and silver, although some of the lower melting solders do contain other alloys such as tin and zinc. Using the compatible solder for the type of metal you are working with means the solder join will be less visible. A specialist flux can be used with gold solders, tenacity no. 5 is recommended for use with metals that require a high melting solder. A specialist solder is also available when working in platinum.

Pickle

After each soldering has taken place, the metal should be placed in a bath of pickle to clean the metal. This is a mixture of sulphuric acid and water in a ratio of one part acid to nine parts water. Always remember to **add the acid to the water** as the other way round can cause an explosion. The container for the pickle must be acid resistant. Pickle containers can be purchased from specialist jewellery suppliers but they are quite expensive. In our workshop we have a household slow cooker which we use exclusively for pickle. It was inexpensive, easy to purchase and keeps the heat constant without making the pickle boil. The pickle works more effectively if it is warm. A Pyrex glass dish heated on a single electric hob is another option.

After a period of time the pickle will stop working, taking a very long time to clean the metal. The term used to describe this is 'spent'.

Other equipment

You will need a good pair of reverse-action insulated tweezers and a pair of standard jeweller's tweezers. Often the piece of solder will move slightly on the metal once it is heated and will need to be pushed back into place. This can be done with a steel or titanium poker. A pair of plastic or brass tweezers will be required when taking the metal in and out of the pickle. Iron binding wire is available in a variety of different thicknesses and is used to hold pieces of metal together when soldering. Also thin iron sheet can be cut into strips and bent round to form clips which hold the metal in place. Always remember to take the wire or clips off before placing in the pickle as it discolours other metals, and turns silver pink. Some experienced jewellers use the reverse-action tweezers to hold the metal together. Soldering can be done on a variety of materials including a charcoal block, soldering wig, soldering sheet or block. Another piece of equipment that is very useful is a revolving soldering stand. This means you can rotate the metal, allowing you to heat the piece evenly.

Soldering metal

You will need:
a basic tool kit for soldering
(see Chapter 2).

1 Make sure the metal to
   be soldered is clean and
   free from grease.
2 Mix up the borax with
   water into a creamy
   lather.
3 With a brush cover the
   area to be soldered with
   the borax paste.

4 Check there are no gaps between the surfaces to be joined – solder will not flow unless every part of the join is touching. Metal sometimes distorts and moves when heated. Even if everything appears to be in place it may be advisable to secure the piece with binding wire or clips to ensure it does not move during soldering.
5 Position the metal on the soldering block. A large piece of work requires a lot of heating. It should be raised off the soldering block to allow the heat to circulate more easily around and underneath the piece. A strip of iron bent into a zigzag shape works well.
6 Cut small pieces of solder with snips and place in the borax dish and cover with borax.
7 Using a pair of fine tweezers, place a small piece of solder next to or on top of the join. If it is a long soldering join, a few pieces may be required.

■ Painting on flux and positioning solder with tweezers.

8 Turn the gas on at the bottle and light the soldering torch with a lighter or match.

9 Gradually heat the area around the join. It is a common mistake for the beginner to heat the solder rather than the surrounding metal. The metal should be heated until it melts the solder which will then flow along the join.

10 Borax tends to bubble when heated, so if the solder moves push it back with your tweezers or a poker. When holding the torch leave your writing hand free for handling the tweezers.

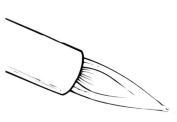
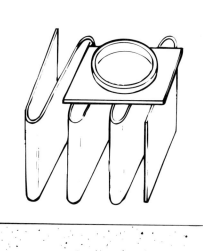

■ Soldering the two metal pieces together.

11 As the metal becomes hotter it will gradually change colour. A red/orange colour indicates that the solder is about to melt. It is important not to heat the metal past soldering as it can also melt.

12 Once soldered, leave to cool, then remove the binding wire or clips and place in the pickle until clean.

13 Take the metal out of the pickle with plastic tweezers and using washing-up liquid and pumice powder clean the surfaces. An old toothbrush or brass brush is great for this.

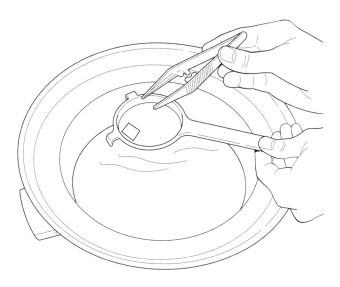

■ Placing soldered piece in pickle with plastic tweezers. A plastic tea strainer keeps small items together.

6

Wire

Wire has always been very popular in jewellery making. It may be used decoratively or to produce simple, lightweight structures. Wire is an easy form of metal to begin working with because it can be manipulated using only hands and some basic tools. To enhance a wire structure, sections can be hammered wider or tapered in and beads or tubes threaded on. It is even possible for wire to be woven, knitted, twisted and crocheted.

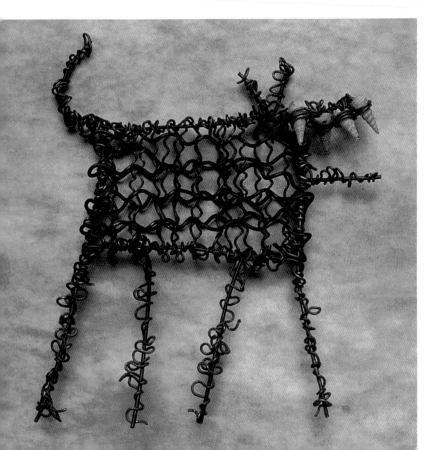

You may find some wire around the home which will be useful to begin experimenting with. Electrical wire contains copper wire beneath the rubber coating. If you peel the coating away this wire is soft and easy to work with. If you buy copper wire from a craft shop check to see if it has a coating. The coating will make it unsuitable for soldering, but it can be fixed in many other ways that do not involve heat, such as twisting, tying or knotting. Iron binding wire is normally used to secure pieces together for soldering, but it is also great for manipulating and weaving. It does not require annealing and holds its shape when bent. Precious metal wire is available in all shapes and sizes from specialist metal suppliers. The section of a wire is the shape of the cross section. Common sections include round, oval, square and D-shaped. D-shaped wire is traditionally used for wedding rings with the flat of the D against the finger. Although these wires can be bought in different sizes many jewellers draw down their own wire.

■ This dog brooch is made from iron binding wire and seashells.

Drawing

Drawing wire involves pulling it through a draw plate which has consecutively smaller holes. When the wire is pulled through smaller and smaller holes it stretches and thins. From one wire it is possible to make a variety of different thicknesses of thinner wire. Draw plates are also available in different shapes so that round wire can be changed to oval wire for example.

To draw wire you will need a draw plate, a vice fixed to something very solid and secure like a heavy bench and some draw plate tongs or mole grips. Draw plate tongs are special tongs that clamp shut with the action of pulling. Their jaws are serrated and one of the handles bends out at the end, preventing your hand from slipping when you pull.

Drawing down wire

You will need: a basic tool kit; draw plate; vice; draw plate tongs; wire; lubricant, such as oil; a joint tool (optional).

1 Anneal the wire. If it is thin, coil it up, securing it with binding wire; this makes it easier to anneal evenly.
2 Straighten the wire by fixing one end in the vice and gripping the other end with serrated pliers so that you can pull hard, keeping it level.

3 Taper one end. If the wire is thin, file the end to a taper. If it is thick, use the wire part of a rolling mill. Feed a few centimetres of the end into the groove closest to the thickness of the wire. To remove the wire again rotate the handle backwards. Move down to the next smallest groove or tighten the mill and repeat the process without feeding quite as much wire through. Continue rolling the wire smaller until the end is tapered. It can be rounded by hammering with a planishing hammer on a steel block, turning the wire as you hit it.
4 Protect the vice with vice protectors or cloth so that the draw plate does not get marked in the vice.
5 Fasten the draw plate into the vice, making sure that all the holes are visible.
6 The front of the draw plate has numbers which correspond to the diameter of the holes and the thickness of the wire it will produce. On the back of the draw plate the holes appear bigger and taper in. Choose the hole one size smaller than the diameter of the wire. Poke the wire in from the back so that the tapered end sticks through to the front. Then grip the tapered end with the tongs and pull it through evenly. Make your action smooth as stopping and starting can mark the wire.
7 Move onto the next size down and repeat the process until you have the desired size or shape. Remember to anneal the wire when it becomes work hardened.

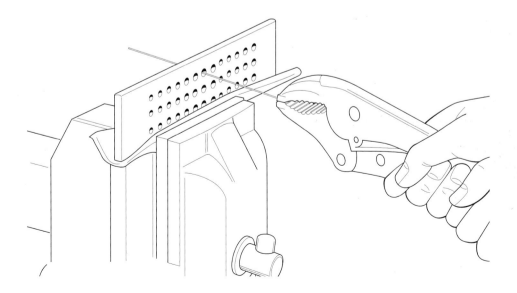

■ Drawing down wire using a draw plate, vice and mole grips.

Bending

If wire is soft and thin the best method of bending it is with your fingers. You can also use your fingers to bend wire round an object such as a pencil. If it cannot be bent this way try annealing the wire first, as this may make it soft enough to work by hand. Pliers need to be used on thicker wire but care must be taken not to mark the metal. To prevent marking use non-serrated pliers and wrap masking tape around the jaws. Round-nosed pliers are used for making tight curves, spirals and loops. Half-round pliers or ring pliers have one flat jaw and one half round. Flat-nosed pliers have two flat jaws, and are used to make sharp bends. Parallel pliers also have flat jaws but they move in a parallel action. They are good for holding work.

Cutting

Thin wire should be cut with snips or wire cutters. Steel wire is so hard that special strong cutters are required. A saw is better for cutting thick wire. To judge the size of the saw blade check that two of the teeth touch the wire at one time.

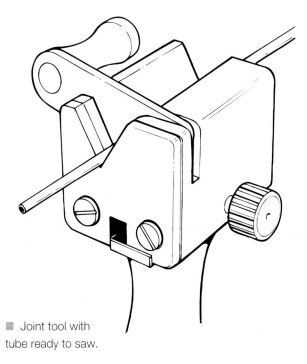

■ Joint tool with tube ready to saw.

A joint tool may be useful to hold the wire and assist sawing in a straight line. A joint tool is a hand-held tool with a channel cut into it to hold a piece of wire or tube. A hinged bar is flipped over the wire to keep it in place and there is a slit in the tool where you saw, helping you to saw straight. Some joint tools have a device which allows the wire to be pushed in a certain distance. This means many pieces of the same length can be cut without measuring each one.

■ Brooch from 18-carat yellow gold wire made with dangling moving hoops.

Spirals

Thin wire can easily be made into a spiral using round-nosed and parallel pliers.

Making a spiral

You will need: a basic tool kit, wire.

1 Anneal the wire.
2 If you wish to make a very tight circle in the centre of the spiral file the end into a taper.
3 Grip the very end of the tapered wire with round-nosed pliers and wind the wire round the jaw of the pliers to make a small circle. To make the circle even smaller use parallel pliers to squeeze it, exerting pressure on the outside of the circle. Squeezing may deform the circle but it can be reshaped using round-nosed pliers or snipe-nosed pliers that have very pointed round ends. The spiral will only be as round as the centre circle.
4 Use parallel pliers to hold the centre circle and, in a twisting action, wind the rest of the wire tightly against this. With each twist move the position of the pliers to allow a better grip and leverage for the next turn.

If the wire is thick it may be too difficult to spiral using only pliers.

Making a spiral using thicker wire

You will need: a basic tool kit; vice; sheet of plastic or metal.

1 In the centre of a flat sheet of plastic or metal, drill a hole the diameter of the wire you are going to use.
2 Anneal the wire and bend it at right angles, about 2 cm from the end of the wire.
3 Push the bent end through the hole. Fasten this end into a vice.
4 Because the wire is firmly gripped in the vice it should be easy to shape the wire into a spiral using the plastic or metal as a flat plate. The first circle will be the hardest to form so you may wish to try forming that before securing it in the vice.
5 When the spiral is made the wire protruding from the bottom can be cut away.

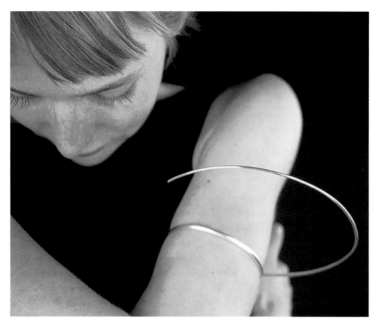

■ Silver arm bracelet by Hannah Keith.

Forging

Forging transforms wire, rod and bar into a flowing line that changes plane and graduates from thick to thin, resembling calligraphy rather than solid metal. Steel hammers stretch, shape and mark the metal. For maximum movement of metal it should be worked on a steel block, anvil or stake. The shape of the hammer head and its position when it hits the surface determine the movement of the metal. A flat-faced or rounded-end hammer hit squarely onto the metal will spread it evenly in all directions. A raising hammer is rectangular shaped with a curved face. If a length of metal is struck along its width with this hammer the metal moves perpendicularly, stretching the metal lengthways. If the metal is struck along its length it will stretch widthways. The metal can also be curved using this hammer. If it is struck along one side rather than centrally the metal on that edge will stretch, making it curve away.

Jump rings

Jump rings are wire rings cut at one point so that they can be opened and linked onto each other to make a chain or join elements together. They can be bought but the best way to get jump rings to fit your particular need is to make them. By making them you have far more choice in the thickness of wire and the size of link.

Making round jump rings

You will need: a basic tool kit; wire.

1   Choose the thickness of wire and anneal it.
2   Find something to form around that has the same diameter as the inside diameter of the jump rings you require. The smooth end of a drill bit is perfect and they are available in many different sizes.
3   Hold one end of the wire with serrated pliers, then using your fingers wrap the other end around the drill bit (or the object you have chosen). Another method is to secure the end of the wire and the drill bit in a vice. For best results wrap tightly, making each coil touch.

4   Each coil equals a jump ring. Push the first few coils off the end of the drill bit and saw down through the middle of them. Make sure that as one ring is cut and falls away the next ring has already been marked by the saw. This locates the saw for the next link to be cut.

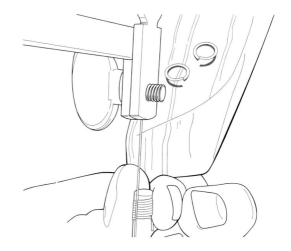

■ Sawing jump rings off wire coil.

5   To open and close the jump rings use two pairs of flat or parallel pliers. Hold the ring with the pliers either side of the saw cut and twist them apart by pulling one side towards you and the other side away. Do not prise them open. This makes it very difficult to close them back into a perfect circle again.

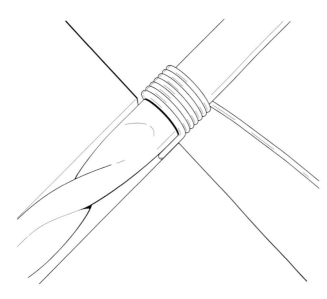

■ Wrapping wire around a drill bit secured in a vice to make jump rings.

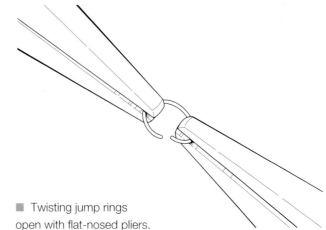

■ Twisting jump rings open with flat-nosed pliers.

Chains

There are a huge variety of chains and most are available to buy from jewellery suppliers. Some are so complex it would be almost unimaginable to hand-make them! It is very time-consuming to make your own chains but in certain circumstances it can be very rewarding. You may only require a small section of chain or one to suit a specific piece of jewellery. A basic chain is made up from jump rings.

Making a simple chain

You will need: a basic tool kit; wire.

1 Make a good number of jump rings using the technique already described.
2 Put aside half and then close the rest by twisting them shut with pliers.
3 Solder the closed links using tiny bits of hard solder. If possible roll the solder very thin in rolling mills to make it easier to cut small pieces. If too much solder is used it has to be cleaned up with a file which can ruin the shape of a link. Also when reheated the links may solder together, making the chain rigid.
4 Take two of the soldered rings and put them onto one of the open links. Close the link and solder it using medium or easy solder. Repeat this with all the other links. The other solder seams can be protected if necessary by painting on rouge to prevent the solder melting again. You may find it faster to set up all the links ready to solder in one go.
5 Next, join groups of three soldered links together with another open link to make seven.
6 Continue in this way until you have the desired length of chain.
7 Pickle the chain once it is completed and clean with a brass brush.

Making a loop-in-loop chain

A loop-in-loop chain is a lovely chain that only involves soldering at the link-making stage.

You will need: a basic tool kit; wire.

1 Make up jump rings and solder them with a small amount of solder.
2 The round jump rings are then made long and oval using round-nosed pliers. Put the nose of the pliers into a jump ring and open them; the action of opening the jaws should stretch the link into a long oval shape.

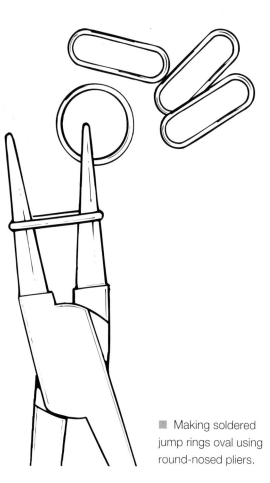

■ Making soldered jump rings oval using round-nosed pliers.

3 Pinch the centre of the oval jump rings closed.
4 When all the links have been shaped, one is bent in half around a scribe or drill bit end so that the two ends touch.

5 Feed the next link through the loops in the first link. If it does not fit easily, open out the loops by pushing the end of a scribe into them. You may need to squash one end of the second link and then open it out again once it is through.

■ The three stages: pinching in the middle, bending and threading through.

6 Once in place, bend the second link in half and then continue adding links until you have reached the desired length of chain.

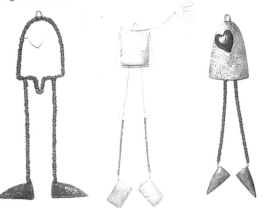

■ Brooches - mixed metals. Some sections are wrapped with wire.

Twisting

Even more variety in wires can be achieved by twisting them. A single square or rectangular wire can be twisted to great effect, but oval and round wires have to be twisted together to achieve a notable difference. Different colours and shapes of wire can also be twisted together in a multitude of ways.

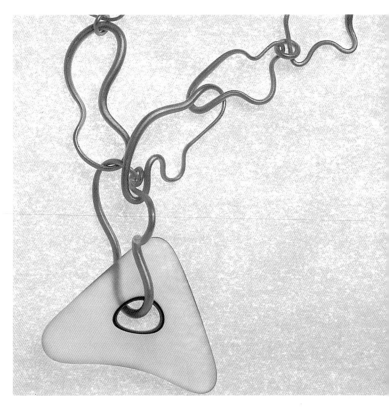

■ Necklace - forged silver wire and American studio glass.

Twisting a single square or rectangular wire

You will need: hand drill; vice; wire.

1 Fix one end of the wire in the vice and the other end in a hand drill where the drill bit would normally go.
2 Turn the handle on the drill. The wire will twist as you turn the handle.
3 Stop when you have the desired effect.

Twisting a wire with itself

You will need: a basic tool kit; hand drill; vice; small hook; wire.

1 Bend a piece of wire in half and put the two ends in the vice.
2 Make a hook and secure it in the hand drill where the drill bit would normally go.
3 Put the loop of wire over the hook and pull it taut, keeping the wire straight.
4 Turn the handle of the drill until the wire has twisted the desired amount.
5 Run solder along the length of the twisted wire to strengthen it before bending or working.

Twisting wires of different shape or colour

You will need: a basic tool kit; hand drill; vice; wire.

1 Solder all the ends together and fix this end in the drill.
2 Fix all the other ends into the vice.
3 Turn the handle of the drill to make the wire twist.

Different coloured wires that have been twisted together then soldered can be drawn through a draw plate just like a plain wire. The result will be a smooth wire with a spiral pattern of colours.

Twisting sections of wire

You will need: a basic tool kit; vice; masking tape; wire.

1 Measure out and mark the length of wire to be twisted.
2 Protect the vice using vice protectors and secure in the wire up to the first mark.
3 Wrap masking tape around the jaws of parallel pliers and grip the wire at the second mark.
4 Twist the pliers to create the twists in the wire.

Filigree

Filigree is an ancient wire technique, in which patterns made of wire are joined together either to make a lightweight see-through structure or to fix to a back plate as surface decoration. In open-work filigree, very fine wire patterns are supported in a thicker wire frame. Filigree patterns can also be soldered to a back plate of metal or fixed with other devices, such as rivets or claws. A combination of the two techniques can also be applied. Only certain parts of the filigree are left open, and this is usually achieved by piercing out sections using a jeweller's saw.

Filigree

You will need: a basic tool kit; charcoal block; wire.

1 A variety of wires can be used for filigree. These can be textured, twisted or beaded, but are usually flattened slightly as this allows the shapes to be pressed against each other more easily within the frame.
2 If the wire is very thin, tweezers may be sufficient to shape it into patterns. For thicker wires, pliers should be used.
3 Nails hammered into a board in certain configurations can be used as a jig to form repeating wire patterns. Snip the heads off the nails so that the pattern can be slipped off easily. In traditional filigree the wires do not overlap. The tension of the swirls and shapes sprung against each other within the thicker wire frame keeps them in place.
4 The wire frame is made of thicker wire and is soldered together using hard solder.
5 The filler units are then soldered in place using medium or easy solder, preferably in one soldering session. As an added measure to secure the wires while soldering, push the prepared filigree into a flattened charcoal block using a flat sheet of metal. The charcoal block will secure the wires and allow the piece to heat more rapidly. Do not use too much solder and try to heat the metal evenly by keeping the flame constantly moving.
6 The filigree is soldered together while flat and then formed into a three-dimensional shape if necessary.

Traditional filigree contains recurring patterns, usually of swirls and sometimes flowers, but filigree can be used to describe any delicate predominantly wire-constructed object. Some modern pieces appear much more spontaneous, like doodles on a page. Wires need not be confined within a thicker wire shape – for added interest some could escape from under the enclosing wire. Experiment with different wires; enamelling cloisonné wire works well because it is already slightly flattened.

Textile techniques

Techniques commonly associated with textiles or basketry can also be applied to jewellery making. If you already have a knowledge of craft techniques, such as knitting, weaving and crochet, these can be directly translated into wire, as long as the wire is thin and malleable enough. The tools are no different from those used with the conventional materials. Knitting needles, a crotchet needle and even a knitting machine can produce successful results. This book does not include lessons on how to knit and crochet, but there are many books on the subject. There is also a whole book devoted to textile techniques in metal if you would like more information. See the end of the book.

There are other textile techniques that do not involve mastering another craft to achieve worthwhile results. The simple techniques of wrapping and binding can be very effective. Wire and metal forms may be wrapped, and also non-metal objects, such as wood and found objects. The technique can be used decoratively or as a form of joining elements together by binding. Sometimes the object is left inside the wrapped wires but it may also be removed by sliding it out or burning it away if the material is suitable.

French knitting

French knitting may be a technique already familiar to you. It is a method for making a knitted tube. I did this as a child using a tool that was made to resemble a wooden doll. Kits containing the necessary equipment for French knitting are sometimes available from toy departments but they are easy to make yourself.

■ Attractive necklaces can be made by shaping wire and tube, and movement introduced by linking components.

Making a French knitting kit

You will need: plastic or wood tube; nails; hammer; snips; fine wire.

1 The main piece of equipment is a ring or short tube made out of a reasonably strong material such as plastic or wood. It is possible to use a thread bobbin.

2 The hole cut out of the centre of the circle determines the diameter of the tube, so take this into consideration if you are using a found object or cutting your own.

3 Nails are hammered in around the edge of the hole. The distance they are from the hole determines the length of the stitches and their closeness together; the number of nails determines the density of the knitting. You should use no fewer than four nails.

4 Remove the heads of the nails so they are no higher than 5 mm and file any sharp edges so they are smooth.

5 You will also need a fine, smooth, metal rod to ease the wire over the pins. This can be made by rounding the end of some 1-mm thick steel wire and polishing it.

6 Fit a handle by pushing the wire into a cork from a wine bottle.

French knitting with wire

You will need: a French knitting ring; wire; metal poker.

1 Wind the wire around each of the pins so that the cross of each loop is in the centre of the ring.

2 Wrap the first pin a second time and then lift the bottom loop over the new loop into the centre of the ring using the metal poker.

3 Repeat this, continuing round in the same direction.

4 The knitting will begin to appear from the bottom of the hoop. You may need to help ease it out at the initial stage.

5 When you have completed the knitting, finish off by threading wire through all the loops.

Experiment with different densities and diameters of knitting until you find the combination you like best. For a slightly different effect keep two loops on the pins and lift the third loop over.

■ Fine chainmail rings made from precious metals.

7

Shaping

One of the exciting aspects of working in metal is that a seemingly hard material can actually be forced into shapes surprisingly easily with the right tools and know-how.

Doming blocks

Flat sheet metal can be domed and formed into hemispheres very easily using a doming block and doming punches. A doming block is a cube made out of brass or steel with variously sized round depressions on each side. For each sized depression there is a corresponding punch with a rounded end that fits the depression perfectly. These punches can be made of wood or metal.

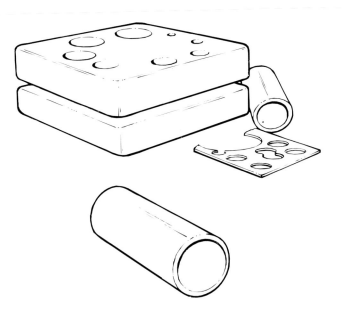

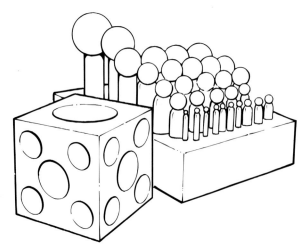

■ Above: Circle cutting tools.

■ Left: Doming block and punches.

Doming metal

You will need: a basic tool kit; doming block and punches; metal.

1   Cut out a circle from a flat sheet of metal. The circle has to be small enough to drop into one of the depressions in the doming block. Circles can be cut by hand using a piercing saw, but if you intend to use a lot of circles, a circle cutter may be useful. A circle cutter is two blocks of steel fixed together in the centre leaving a gap between them. Various sized holes go right through the two blocks. Each has a cutter consisting of a rod of metal with a sharp-edged circular bottom. The metal to be cut is slid in-between the two blocks making sure there is metal under the size of hole required. The correct sized cutter is then dropped into the hole to rest on the metal. Check you have the cutter the correct way up with the sharp-edged end in the block touching the metal. The top of the cutter is hit hard with a hammer so that it goes through the metal making the circle fall out of the bottom.

2   Anneal the circle of metal.

3   Place the circle in a depression in the doming block. Position the corresponding punch in the depression on top of the circle. Hit the punch, with a hammer if it is metal and a mallet if the punch is wooden. It is important to use the correct sized punch. Check that it fits snugly in the hole before you hit it – both the block and the punches will be damaged if the wrong sized punch is used.

4   The first hit of the punch will dome the metal slightly. Then place in the next smallest indentation, changing the punch to fit, and hit it again. Continue to move the metal into smaller and smaller depressions until the metal has domed into a hemisphere or the domed shape you require.

5   Two domes can be soldered together to create a sphere or bead. Before soldering, a small hole must be drilled in one of the sections to allow hot air inside to escape. After the bead has been pickled in acid, it should be boiled in sodium bicarbonate solution followed by water to neutralize the acid which will have seeped inside the bead.

■ These rings made from precious metals by Lois Brodie demonstrate the domed shapes that can be created using a die.

Dies

Cushioned three-dimensional forms of all shapes and sizes can be made using a die. Although dies can be quite complicated, like casting, undercutting and sharp differences in depth are not possible. Conforming dies involve two parts, male and female, which fit together exactly. The female part is indented and the male part protruding. This type of die is used to produce identical items in large quantities. Non-conforming dies are easier to make in the workshop. They reproduce the outline of a shape but the depth and form of the piece can be altered every time the die is used.

Dies are useful if you wish to make corresponding parts. If the die is turned over and an impression is also taken from the other side, the two impressions will fit together perfectly, producing a hollow form. They are also useful for production pieces because the same shape can be reproduced.

Making a die

You will need: a basic tool kit; MDF or thick plastic; steel (optional); metal.

Safety
Wear a mask when cutting MDF and plastic.

1　To make a die out of MDF or thick plastic, cut out a rectangle or a square quite a bit larger than you require.
2　Draw the shape onto the MDF or plastic and drill a hole inside the drawn line so that the saw blade fits through. Cut out the shape without cutting the surrounding MDF or plastic which is the support for the metal.
3　Try to saw vertically so that the shape underneath is the same size as it is on the top. This will prevent the metal touching the edges and denting when it is pushed down. It will also make it easier to take an opposite impression from the bottom that will exactly fit an impression taken from the top.
4　For a more defined edge to the shape a sheet of steel with the corresponding shape cut out can be fixed onto the plastic or wood. This also makes the die stronger. The steel can be turned over and used on the other side of the die for an opposite impression.

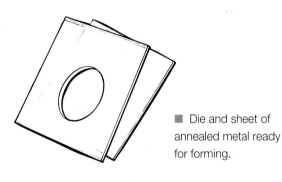

■ Die and sheet of annealed metal ready for forming.

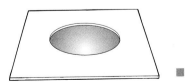

■ Formed shape.

Using a die with a fly press

A fly press is a large mechanical machine which exerts pressure on a block of rubber, pushing it into the metal and die, creating an even smooth pillow form. A sheet of metal allowing at least a 2 cm edge surrounding the shape should be cut and annealed. It is then fixed securely to the die using masking tape. This is placed on a steel block under the weight of the fly press with the metal facing up. Blocks of rubber of different hardness are placed on top of the metal; the softer the rubber, the deeper the indent will be. Another block of steel is placed on top of this sandwich. The fly press is wound around, lifting the weight and then pushing back in the opposite direction so that the weight falls down on the die and metal. This can be repeated if you want a deeper depression. Instead of rubber, Blu-Tack can be used as an alternative. This is especially effective for small designs.

A fly press is a piece of machinery that only large workshops and colleges may have. If you don't have access to one you can still use a hand-made die.

■ Brooch of precious metals showing fly-pressed shape.

Using a die without a fly press

You will need: a basic tool kit; die; sheet of steel; metal; masking tape; vice.

1　Anneal the metal and secure it to the die with masking tape.
2　Put a blob of Blu-Tack in the centre of the metal where the shape will be made and place a similar sized sheet of steel over this. Fix the whole sandwich into a vice.
3　Tighten the vice until the die and metal squash together. When it is removed the metal should have domed into the shape of the die. If it has not domed enough try again with more Blu-Tack.

Repoussé and chasing

Safety

- *White spirit and paraffin are flammable liquids – keep away from naked flames.*
- *Do not overheat the pitch because the fumes created are very unpleasant.*

Repoussé and chasing are methods of creating relief designs from flat sheet metal using punches. Repoussé involves working from the back of a design to create the initial shape, using big punches for deeper shapes. Chasing is predominantly carried out from the front of the work, and different punches are used to add detail and definition and to finalize the piece.

To allow the metal to shape and move it must be supported in a material which will move with it and cushion the hammer blows. For very low relief chasing wet leather or hardwood may be adequate as a support. For work which involves any depth, a special pitch mixture is the ideal medium. The pitch is mixed with brick dust or plaster of Paris to stiffen the mixture. Tallow or linseed oil is then added to soften the pitch and give it more plasticity. These can be combined in various ratios depending on how hard or soft you require the pitch to be. In cold weather, pitch becomes more brittle and extra linseed oil may be required. The pitch is poured into a cast-iron bowl. This can be half-filled with concrete if you do not have enough pitch. Pitch can be bought from specialist jewellery suppliers in a block which can be broken up with a hammer and melted into the bowl. Melt pitch in a well-ventilated area, taking care not to overheat it. The bowl is extremely heavy and is supported in a ring of rope, leather or metal so that it is steady but easy to move into all different angles for ease of working.

The punches required for chasing and repoussé are all different shapes and sizes. Some metalworkers make their own out of hardened steel so they can have the exact shape required for a certain job. To begin with a small selection of bought punches will be sufficient; the doming punches with a doming block can be used for repoussé.

There are a number of different types of chasing punches. Tracing punches are used to create lines. They are often used first to outline the design on the front of the metal. Embossing punches are larger and rounded and are used next to create the initial depth and shape. They are usually worked from the back of a piece. Planishing punches are used to smooth off the finished surface. Matting punches have a texture imprinted on the end and this is transferred to the metal, creating textures. All the punches have slightly rounded edges to prevent cutting and digging into the metal. These are all highly polished except for the matting punches because the definition of the texture would be lost through polishing.

When chasing, attention must be centred on the punches and the marks they are making rather than on the point where the hammer makes contact with the punch. A special hammer is used with a round, flat head. The larger surface area makes it easier to hit the punch. The chasing hammer also has a special handle which is thin from the head of the handle and bulbous at the end, making it very springy and easy to hold.

■ Brooch with chased dog and enamel background.

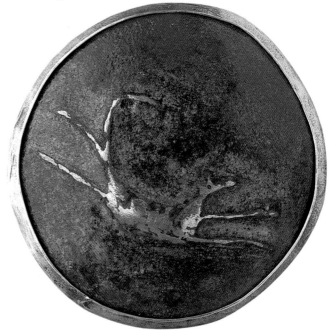

Chasing

You will need: a basic tool kit; bowl of pitch; chasing or doming punches; chasing hammer; sheet metal; paraffin or white spirit.

1 During the chasing process the metal is stretched quite considerably. Copper and silver are good metals to work with because they are very malleable. Choose a piece of metal between 0.6 mm and I mm thick, depending on the depth of the chasing. The metal will tear if it is too thin or if it has not been annealed when necessary. Uneven and vigorous chasing can also cause ruptures. These should be repaired immediately by flooding the area from the back with a matching coloured hard solder. If the area is larger, patch it with a small piece of the same metal, then file away the edges to make it flush with the rest of the piece.

2 Cut a rectangle or square of metal allowing at least a 1-cm border around the design you intend to chase.

3 Anneal the metal.

4 With a pair of pliers bend three of the corners down, these will help to secure the metal in the pitch. Bend the last corner up in the opposite direction. This will be used as a grip when pulling the metal out for annealing or turning over.

5 Grease or place masking tape over the side of the metal which will be placed face down into the pitch. This will make it easier to remove and clean.

6 Warm the pitch with a soft flame, taking care not to bubble or burn it. It gives off horrible fumes and once burnt is useless to work with.

7 Scrape some of the softer pitch into the centre of the bowl so that when you press the metal onto the mound of pitch it will squeeze out from underneath. This should reduce the chance of air bubbles. Push the metal into the soft pitch so that the three corners dig in. All the metal must make contact with the pitch. If there is a trapped air bubble the chasing punch will bounce off and have no effect, or will dent the metal in an unexpected way. It will be obvious if you have hit an air bubble because the sound of impact will be dull. Remove the metal and try to position it again with no air trapped underneath.

■ Metal pushed into warm pitch. Use a wet finger to secure in place.

8 When the metal is in place and while the pitch is still soft, wet your fingers and push some of the pitch over the edges of the metal to hold it securely in place. If you get hot pitch stuck to your fingers wait until it cools. To remove it, run your fingers under a cold tap.

9 The design can now be drawn onto the metal using a permanent marker or, if you are copying a design, using tracing paper.

10 Use a tracer punch to make the design outline permanently visible from both sides of the metal. Hold the punch at an angle so that it moves towards you when hit. The tapping and moving of the punch should be smooth and not jerky, producing a continuous line rather than a series of dashes. It will take practice to be able to follow your drawn lines with the punch.

■ Chasing using a punch and hammer.

11 Once the outline has been chased the metal is removed from the pitch by heating both the metal and pitch gently. Pull it out by the corners using pliers.

12 If the pitch has stuck to the metal, clean it off by soaking in white spirit or paraffin. Scrub stubborn bits off with an old toothbrush.

13 If you want to continue work on the piece, anneal the metal and put it back in the pitch the other way up. Remember you will have to change the direction of some of the bent corners.

14 The design outline will now appear raised because the metal has been turned over. Embossing or doming punches are now used to create depth in the design. You will find it easier to work if the pitch is still slightly soft. The embossing punches should always be kept moving as they are being hit, this prevents a lumpy surface. Depth is not made by hitting the punch very hard but by firmly tapping the punch while moving it backward, forward and around the area you wish to stretch.

15 To see what your design looks like without removing the metal from the pitch push some Plasticine into the chasing; the design will become imprinted into the Plasticine.

16 Remember to remove and anneal the metal when it becomes work hardened.

17 When the metal begins to take shape you may find the surrounding metal has also begun to move and bend. Before placing it back in the pitch flatten it again. Make a punch out of a small block of hardwood. The punch should be quite flat but with the edges rounded off so you can flatten the metal close to your design without marking it. Clean and anneal the metal, and place it the right way up on a steel block. Flatten as much of the surrounding metal as you can using a mallet, taking care not to hit and dent your design.

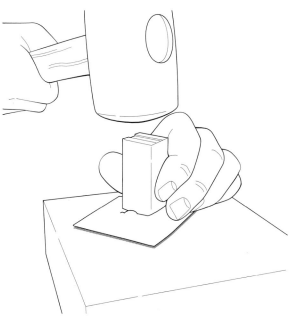

■ Remove from pitch and flatten surrounding metal using a wooden block and mallet.

18 When the metal is worked it begins to take on a more three-dimensional form. This means that before more work is carried out to the front of the piece, the hollow must be filled with pitch to ensure there are no air bubbles. Breaking off chunks of pitch, place them in the chased-out hollow. Hold the metal with some long tongs and gently warm the underside with a torch until the pitch melts and fills all the crevices. Keep adding lumps until there is enough pitch to fill the hollow, level with the rest of the metal. Once the pitch has cooled and stiffened, the piece can be turned over and placed in the pitch bowl as usual.

19 Once you have completed chasing, the surrounding metal may be cut away. Flatten the metal as before, then saw out your design following the outline. File the edges and smooth with emery paper to remove sharp edges. You will find the structure is very strong.

Chasing is a great method for creating three-dimensional images in metal. Detail, depth and undercut can be introduced, making it a much more flexible technique than stamping or using a die. Don't be put off by the messy aspect of the pitch. After some practice it is very satisfying watching the metal move and the design emerge. The technique really takes advantage of the malleability of metal and it is amazing that a material so seemingly hard can be moulded in such a way.

Very thin sheets of copper and brass can be bought in rolls. This is called shim. If the shim is annealed and placed on a soft surface, such as wood or leather, it can be drawn on using a scribe and the design will be in relief on the other side. Because this is such a simple technique, intricate patterns can be drawn, although only a little depth can be introduced. The metal is very soft and thin, so once drawn on it may have to be fixed to something stronger.

Scoring and bending

Although metal can be bent into an angle using parallel pliers, the corner will not be sharp but rounded. To achieve a very sharp corner the metal must be scored, working on the same principle as scoring card or paper. If the metal is quite thick you will need special scoring tools. These are often made using the butt of an old file. The butt is bent at right angles and the end is ground down into an angled sharp cutting tool. The angle of the tool determines the angle of the bend, so that if the tool is right-angled the bend will be right-angled too.

For most small jewellery work, a scribe and a square or triangular file are all that are required to score lines to fold up into a rectangle or square.

■ Neckpiece – mixed metals. Lovely beads can be made by joining two domed sections together.

Making a strip of metal into a square or rectangle

You will need: a basic tool kit; strip of metal.

1 Calculate the sides of the rectangle or square required. Mark these measurements onto a strip of metal, allowing a tiny amount of extra material for each side.

2 Score the four points across the width of the strip using a scribe or a saw blade. Ensure that the lines scored are not squint.

3 Cut along the fourth score line.

4 File the two ends of the strip at a 45° angle.

5 Use a square needle file to file metal away from the scored lines until a faint line is visible from the back.

6 The strip can then be easily bent up into a right angle using flat or parallel pliers. Once the shape is made it is secured with binding wire and all of the corners are strengthened by soldering.

7 It can now be soldered onto a back plate if desired.

Making a ring

A ring can be formed on a round triblet. To work out the length of metal you will need there is a simple equation.

You will need: a basic tool kit; ring triblet; ring gauge.

1 Select a ring from the ring gauge that fits your finger.

2 Measure the diameter of the chosen ring with a ruler.

3 Multiply this number by π and add on twice the thickness of the metal you are using. This will give you the exact length of wire or metal to cut.

4 Shape this length around a ring triblet and solder the two ends together.

5 Reshape and finish to your satisfaction.

■ Box brooches – oxidized silver and gold with moving components.

8

Textures and surface finishes

At the design stage think about how you want the finished piece of jewellery to look. High-street jewellery is often smooth and highly polished, but this does not have to be the case. Textures and patterns on the metal surface create wonderful and exciting effects. Polished and satin finishes combined together with a texture can look stunning.

With most designs the texture or pattern will have to be done first on a flat sheet of metal before any forming, shaping or piercing has taken place. The addition of texture onto a shaped surface will cause distortion and, in most cases, will alter the shape of the piece. The surface finishes are the final step after texturing, soldering and filing have been completed.

If you are unsure of the texture or finish you require, then experiment on some test pieces. Keep a small sketchbook of all the samples with a record of how you achieved each one. Sometimes it will be impossible to recreate exactly the same effect but at least the initial reference material is available.

■ Silver earrings and matching brooch. Gimp (normally used when stringing necklaces) creates the fascinating texture.

Roll-printing

To roll-print a texture onto metal you will need a set of rolling mills. These are expensive, but are a valid piece of equipment in any jeweller's workshop. In our workshop we have a set of mini mills which are ideal for small pieces of jewellery. Roll-printing is an easy technique for producing interesting textures.

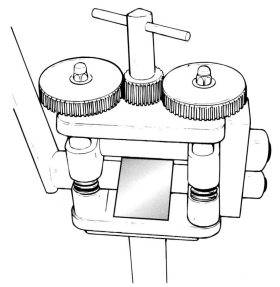

◼ A set of rolling mills used for roll printing with a sheet of metal being fed through.

Items that are great for roll-printing onto metal include string, various papers, feathers, leaves, sandpaper, fine wire, wire mesh and even a strand of hair! The two rollers are made from stainless steel and, although they are strong, they need to be looked after: any metal passing through could be embossed with an unwanted scratch or dent caused by a mark on the rollers. Make sure the item to be embossed onto the metal is quite flat and soft enough to go through the rollers. Iron binding wire will mark the rollers, but to prevent this it can be sandwiched between a sheet of stainless steel and the metal. The rollers are tightened so that the pressure embosses the texture onto the metal surface as it is fed through.

How to roll-print

You will need: a basic tool kit; rolling mills; embossing material; metal.

1 Make sure the metal to be embossed is not too thick. Something between 0.4 mm and 0.8 mm is good to start with. The metal has to be soft so anneal it first and clean in the pickle. Then wash it in water and towel dry. Avoid getting water on the rollers, as they will go rusty.

2 Place the metal and embossing material at the edge of the rollers and gently turn the handle. If the metal is not budging then slightly loosen the rollers, if the metal passes through too easily tighten the rollers.

3 There has to be a certain amount of pressure for the item passing through to become embossed onto the metal surface, but you will discover this when you experiment.

Etching

Safety

◼ *Always wear protective goggles, clothing and rubber gloves when working with nitric acid as it is extremely strong and will burn your skin as well as clothes.*

◼ *If, for any reason, acid gets into your eyes, then wash immediately with eyewash and seek medical help.*

◼ *The acid needs to be mixed and used in a well-ventilated area. An extractor system is the best method, but next to a wide open window or outside is adequate.*

◼ *Always add acid to water.*

◼ *Store acid in a safe place in a labelled bottle.*

◼ *Dispose of all acids safely. Contact your local council if you need advice.*

Etching can be a very effective way of making marks in metal and is a straightforward technique once you have acquired the right equipment. Etching is a technique where the metal is placed in a diluted bath of nitric or sulphuric acid which eats down into the metal surface. The longer the metal stays in the acid, the larger the grooves will become. The acid not only works down into the metal, but also spreads to either side, creating a deeper, thicker line.

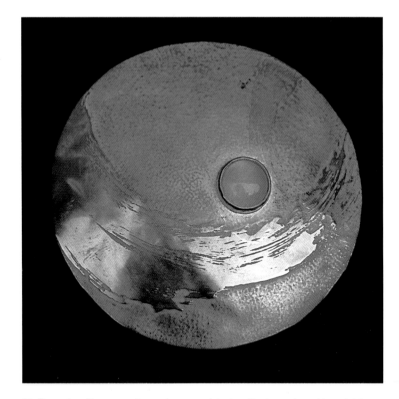

■ Brooch with moonstone shows painterly effect produced by etching.

Resist

Both sides of the metal are covered in resist so that only the areas exposed to the acid solution will etch. Resist comes in a variety of forms, and the one most commonly used is called stop-out varnish. Another is a block of wax, called soft or hard ground. These products can be purchased from specialist stockists.

Applying resist

You will need: stop-out varnish and hard or soft ground; reverse-action tweezers; a flame; scribe or sharp tool.

1   The metal must be clean and grease-free on both sides. Use pumice powder, washing-up liquid or a fine-grade emery paper to achieve this.

2   If you are just using varnish as your resist, this can be painted on one side of the metal, left to dry, and then painted on the other side.

3   If you are using both the varnish and the hard or soft ground, first heat the metal so it is warm, but not to an annealing temperature, then gradually coat the top surface, melting on the hard or soft ground, and leave to dry. The underside can then be covered with the varnish.

4   To transfer a design onto the metal, scribe into the resist until the metal is showing once again. Blunt tools can be used to draw into the soft ground but the varnish is good for scribing fine lines. The design can be as complex or as simple as you require – wherever the metal is showing, that is where the acid will etch.

Etching fluid

It is important to dilute the nitric acid before etching or it will be far too strong and will cause the metal to dissolve. Always remember to add the acid to the water. This is extremely important, as an explosion of violent splattering and fumes can occur if the process is carried out the other way round. Use a Pyrex glass dish or a plastic container, such as an old ice-cream container, to mix the acid and water. Remember to label it well and do not use it for anything else.

Solution strengths can vary for different metals. A general strength of nine parts water to one part acid for silver, brass, copper and steel is recommended. This is a fairly weak solution but it will give you a rough guide to how fast your metals are etching. More acid can be added if the solution is not working. For a very fast etch try a ratio of one part water to one part nitric acid. This is a strong mix so watch the metal carefully, checking that the resist does not begin to peel off. The correct strength of the acid is something you will be able to gauge as you experiment with the technique. It is a good idea to use different containers for each metal and label the strength of acid and water and how long it takes to etch the finish you require.

Plastic tweezers or plastic tea strainers are ideal to lift the metal in and out of the acid solution. Try not to be too impatient, it may take anything from ten minutes to over an hour to achieve the etch you want. If the acid works too quickly it can produce an uneven etch, and the resist will come away from the metal, leaving it exposed to the acid.

As with pickle, etching acid becomes 'spent' over a period of time. This means it will no longer etch the metal and a new batch will need to be made up. There is no easy way to dispose of the acid, but pouring a small amount at a time down a drain with plenty of water is probably the safest; alternatively contact your local council. It is easy enough to tell if the acid solution is working, as tiny bubbles will appear on the surface of the metal. If the bubbles are too furious then the acid is too strong. To rectify this, place another one or two parts of water into a separate container and then transfer the already mixed solution into this. Use a feather to tickle the top of the metal surface to remove the bubbles, which can cause an uneven etch. Remember the acid does not just etch downwards, but also undercuts forming a thicker line. This can also happen if the acid is a stronger solution. Make sure the metal is taken out of the acid quite frequently and washed under the tap. Take a pin or jeweller's scribe across the etched line to judge the depth.

The resist can be removed using paraffin. Let the metal soak in a small amount first, then using an old toothbrush rub over the surface until all the resist has been removed. Washing-up liquid with water also helps to remove any excess varnish or wax. This process can be very messy so wear rubber gloves.

Acid to water mixing guide

General mix (light/slow etch) Water 4–9 parts to nitric acid 1 part

Copper, brass and steel (faster etch) Water 1 part to nitric acid 1 part or water 2 parts to sulphuric acid 1 part

Silver (strong solution) Water 1 part to nitric acid 2–3 parts

Silver (weaker solution) Water 3–5 parts to nitric acid 1 part

The more acid added to the water the stronger the solution, therefore it will work faster and produce a stronger etch. Try not to mix up more acid than you actually need.

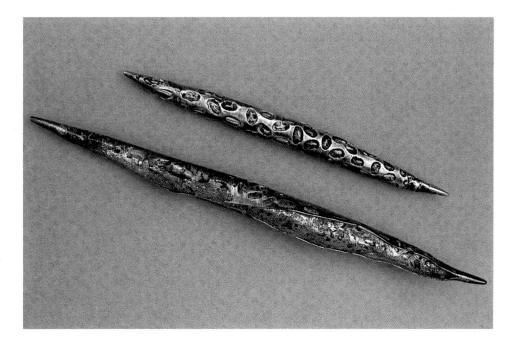

■ These brooches have been shaped and etched very deeply. They are made in silver with the addition of gold leaf.

Punches and hammer marks

Various punches and hammers when used on metal can make very interesting marks and textures. All hammers will make some sort of mark on metal. When hammering onto metal make sure your work is supported by something heavy and flat. Steel blocks are great for this and can be purchased in a variety of sizes. Although these can fit on top of the workbench you might be lucky enough to acquire an old tree trunk or a solid piece of wood to work on. These are more solid and less noisy to hammer on. Old hammers with lots of wear and tear are engraved with marks and rust which give interesting effects when hammered onto a metal surface. You may have some going rusty at home, but look out for them also at car-boot sales and junk shops. Try hammering wires or mesh into annealed metal. It might not be as defined as the roll-printing or etching techniques but a subtle effect could be just what you are looking for.

Punches

All jeweller's punches will have some sort of patterned or shaped end that can be used to texture metal. The punches are usually quite small lengths of steel but are heavy enough to form marks when hit with a hammer. Punches that are used for chasing can also be used for texturing metal. Specialist punches can be made to stamp your initials into the metal and for hallmarking, which states the type of precious metal.

Abrasive finishes

Papers

Different grades of wet and dry and emery papers can produce various finishes when rubbed against the metal surface. The finer grades of paper are usually used to polish the metal. Try using the paper in a circular motion rather than in the same direction for a different effect. The various grades of paper can produce a scratchy appearance or something quite subtle.

Try the same techniques with a brass or wire brush, as this will also give the metal a scratched polished surface. Experimentation with various types of pan scourers and wire steel wool could be something else to try. Even some abrasive kitchen and bathroom cleaners will produce marks on metal.

Wet and dry paper Roughest 240, 320, 360, 400, 600, 800, 1000, 1200 Finest

Emery paper Roughest 3, 2, 1, 1C, 1M, 1F, 0, 2/0, 3/0, 4/0, 7/0 Finest

Sheets of paper are usually sold in dimensions 280 × 230 mm (11"x 9") and can be purchased singly or in assorted packs that consist of various grades.

Pumice powder

Pumice powder can be purchased from jewellery suppliers and is used as a cleaning agent to rid the metal surface of dirt and grease. It is used with water and an old toothbrush, brass brush, cloth or finger. It also creates a subtle scratched satin finish surface on the metal, which for some designs can look very attractive.

Oxidization

Safety
- *Work in a well-ventilated area.*
- *Wear rubber gloves and protective goggles.*

Oxidization occurs on the surface of copper, bronze, brass and silver if it is exposed to sulphur which is present in the air. The metal turns black and needs to be cleaned with either a polishing cloth or a cleaning agent like silver dip. In some cases the black appearance is intentional, as in the work by Anna Gordon. See photographs on pages 21 and 47.

To achieve this effect the piece has to be placed in a diluted solution of liver of sulphur. This chemical works best when it has been warmed slightly. Dilute the required amount with hot water and use immediately or mix in cold water and place the jar in a bowl of hot water so it warms up gradually. The liver of sulphur solution will blacken metals such as silver, copper and 9ct and 14ct gold.

For the solution mix 22 g of liver of sulphur with 1 litre of warm water. If the colour is too grey then add some more liver of sulphur until you achieve the required black. As the liver of sulphur comes in lumps it is easy to break off and add a little at a time. The blackening can peel away from the surface if the metal is greasy or the solution is too strong. Remember to wear gloves when working with this chemical and use in a well-ventilated area, as it is very smelly!

■ The beads on these rings all swivel. The ring on the left is patterned with spots using a punch from behind and etched.

Patination

Patination with copper nitrate

Copper nitrate is a chemical that turns the metal surface a blue/green colour when heated. This process can be achieved using a jeweller's torch.

To produce a blue/green patina mix 200 g of copper nitrate with 1 litre of water. Make sure the metal surface is free from dirt and grease, using pumice powder, fine emery paper or washing-up liquid with an old toothbrush to achieve this. The metal surface is heated with a torch and the solution is then applied with a soft brush until it covers the metal with an even blue/green patina. If the surface is then heated without further application of the solution, it will become black. The solution may then be applied to the black ground, heating the metal again to form the blue/green patina. The end result varies depending on how the solution has been applied. A spotty, speckled appearance can be achieved using the solution with a dry brush, trailing it across the metal surface. A marble effect is produced if the metal becomes caked with the solution. When you have reached your final finish you must leave the piece to cool down and dry out; do not quench in water or place in the pickle. Once dried a wax finish can be added or a special lacquer sprayed on.

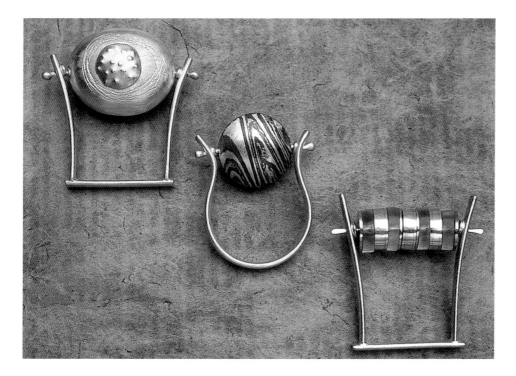

Plating

The plating process removes a layer from one metal, distributing it onto the surface of another, thus changing its appearance. Usually it is a more precious alloy of metal that is plated onto a less precious one, for example copper would be plated with silver, silver would be plated with either 9ct, 18ct or 24ct gold.

The equipment needed to plate metal is very expensive and is not recommended for use outside a professional workshop. The chemicals used for plating are very toxic and should only be used by someone who has had specialist training. An area has to be built for this process with extractor fans and specialist equipment.

If however you like the idea of plating metal, there are now easy-to-use substances on the market. They are perfectly safe as long as you wear the protective gloves provided and follow the instructions carefully. The silver plating solution is available at most large department stores. It is simply rubbed onto the surface like a polish.

Leafing

Gold and silver leaf is a beautiful way of adding that extra little something to a piece, creating surface decoration and making it look expensive. See photograph opposite.

The leaf comes in platinum, silver and different carats of gold in a variety of thicknesses. It is also possible to buy leaf in gold, silver and copper colours. Copper foil is actual copper but the gold and silver do not contain any silver or gold alloys.

Gold and silver leaf does not only have to be used on metal, but also works well on other materials, such as wood, stone, plastic and paper. Gold and silver leaf can be purchased in small books with sheets of the leaf slotted into each sleeve.

To apply the leaf you need a special substance called size. This is a translucent adhesive, which holds the leaf in place, like glue. Size is available with different lengths of drying time that can vary from one hour to 24 hours. The size has to be applied with a fine brush to the desired area and then left for a little while before placing on the leaf. It should feel slightly tacky, so test the surface gently with your little finger to see what stage it is at.

Transfer gold leaf is attached to a piece of fine paper and is easy to apply to the jewellery. Shapes can be cut out with scissors, making it easier to work with. Loose leaf requires more control as it has a tendency to float away. For loose leaf use a brush to transfer it from the book to the object. The friction from the brush to the leaf is usually enough to lift it, but if you are having difficulties then a tiny amount of petroleum jelly on the end of the brush should help. Once the leaf has made contact, press down gently making sure the brush doesn't touch the size. It is possible the leaf could tear slightly, but this can be covered up with a second layer. Once dry, the surface can be burnished with a cotton-wool ball or soft cloth. Any leaf that comes away has not stuck properly and needs to be reapplied. Any unwanted size can be removed with white spirit and a brush, tissue or cotton-wool bud. Brushes can also be cleaned using white spirit.

■ Right: silver, paper, 18-carat yellow gold, Perspex and gold leaf brooch.

Polishing

Hand-polishing

Hand-polishing metal is just as effective as using machinery, however it is more time-consuming. Sometimes, because of the delicacy or shape of a piece, polishing by hand is the only way to achieve the desired effect. When polishing by hand you will need to go through a variety of stages until reaching the final finish. This can be separated into two stages: the first is polishing which gets rid of all the scratches and gives the metal an all over finish; the second stage gives the metal its highly polished appearance and is termed buffing or burnishing.

Making a polishing stick

You will need: a basic tool kit; a wooden or plastic stick approximately 300 mm (12") long, 5 mm ($^1/_8$") thick and 20 mm (8") wide; abrasive paper.

1   Abrasive papers include wet and dry papers, emery and rouge paper. Taking your abrasive papers, on the reverse side mark out and score the four folding points.
2   Leave a small section around the bottom free to hold the stick and use the glue to attach the abrasive paper all the way round the stick, making sure it is really tight.
3   Make a variety of sticks using different grades of abrasive papers for different finishes.

For final polishing, the sticks can be covered with chamois leather or felt. These should be used in conjunction with the appropriate polishing compounds, Tripoli polish and then rouge.

■ Coiled necklace of silver wire circles, roll printing, paper and gold plating.

Abrasive tape or cord

Tape or cord is impregnated with an abrasive substance on both sides and can be cut to any length to fit the area you are working on. It is another effective method for hand-polishing and is great for getting into those difficult small areas and holes if used like dental floss.

Steel wool

Steel wool can be purchased in a variety of grades from coarse to fine. Use in a circular motion or in an up/down motion so that all the scratches go in the same direction.

Brass brushes

Brass brushes come in a variety of grades. They give the metal surface a scratched but shiny appearance.

Polishing cloths

These are impregnated with polishing compound and tarnish remover. They can be used directly onto the metal, but the piece will need to be washed thoroughly in hot soapy water after polishing.

Metal polish for brass and silver

This polish comes as a liquid that can be used straight from the bottle with a clean soft cloth or rag. Again, wash the piece in hot soapy water when you have finished polishing and dry carefully, making sure you do not scratch the surface. Wear household rubber gloves as the polish can irritate the skin.

Burnishing

Burnishing is the final treatment in the polishing process. The metal is made shiny by rubbing it with hardened, tempered steel giving a smooth, highly polished finish. Burnishers usually come in lengths of 3 to 4 inches (75–100mm) and are attached to a wooden handle making them comfortable to hold. The steel is very hard and smooth, so when rubbed against jewellery it will not mark it, but will create a polished appearance. It is necessary to use a lubricant to stop the metal dragging as you burnish. Either soapy water or washing-up liquid in water is ideal. Dip the

burnisher in the soapy solution before starting, and make sure the work is free from dust. Use the burnisher in one direction to avoid streakiness, making sure you place your jewellery on a cloth, piece of felt or leather so it does not slip. Rub over the whole piece with a soft cloth. When all the burnishing is complete make sure the tool is dry to prevent it rusting and rub it with a candle to cover in wax.

Barrel polishing

Tumbling, small, smooth shots of steel in a rotating barrel along with a piece of jewellery will give the surface a highly polished finish. The barrel, or tumble polisher, can be purchased from specialist stockists and will include a motorized unit plus a lidded barrel. The cheaper models are usually made from rubber and are ideal for use in a small workshop. The barrel moves mechanically in a rotating manner and the metal shots burnish the jewellery making it shiny.

■ Barrel polisher, barrelling compound and steel shots.

The tumbling shot is made from hardened tempered steel and comes in different shapes, which include round, bullet, pins, diagonally cut, cylinder sections and diamond shapes. Barrelling compound in powder form has to be added to the barrel along with water to make a soapy solution. This helps to lubricate the shots over the piece of jewellery and also prevents the steel shots from going rusty. When you are not using the barrel, dry off the shots and keep them in a jar or plastic bag so they are moisture-proof. Also available are cutting cones or ceramic chips which make the metal surface turn matt, creating a satin finish.

Pendant drill

Safety
- *Wear protective goggles.*
- *Tie back loose hair and clothing.*

A pendant drill with small head attachments is ideal for polishing difficult pieces, such as the insides of rings. The pendant drill is ideal for use in a small workshop as it doesn't take up much room and can be used at the workbench. The pendant drill hangs off a bracket from the wall or a low ceiling. A specially designed stand which bolts onto the workbench can also be purchased from suppliers. The pendant drill works by placing

pressure on a foot pedal and, just like working a sewing machine, the more pressure put onto the pedal the faster the motor will rotate. They are not only good for polishing but with the right head attachments can also be used for drilling and burring.

The head attachments for polishing come in the form of emery papers, steel, brass, felt, wool, calico, leather and rubber. Used with the right polishing compound the metal will be brought up to a high shine or satin appearance. The heads are available in a variety of strengths, including hard, medium, soft or abrasive finish. When you are using the pendant drill make sure that you support the work firmly with one hand on the bench, and use a leather cloth or some Plasticine to stop the work from sliding. This leaves the other hand free to work the pendant drill.

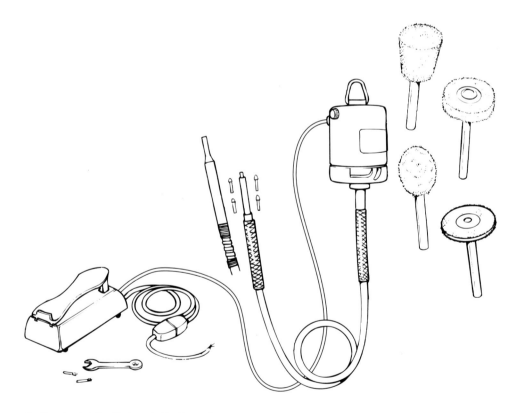

Pendant drill with head attachments.

Polishing motor

Safety

- *Wear protective goggles.*
- *Tie back loose hair and clothing.*

A polishing motor consists of one or two arms known as spindles onto which different mop heads can be attached. The mop heads come in a variety of forms which include calico, wool, felt, steel, brass and abrasive finishes. Surround the back and sides of the polishing motor with a wooden box to prevent polish and fluff from the mop flying off and creating dust around the workshop. The spindles rotate very quickly so make sure you keep loose hair and jewellery out of the way and always wear protective goggles.

Once the machine is turned on, press the polishing compound hard against the mop until it is covered in a good layer of polish. Then, line up the work and gradually push up against the mop, turning the piece with each stoke. Keep the piece moving against the mop and avoid staying on the same bit too long, as it will gradually wear down the surface. If you want a crisp edge take care not to overpolish that area. The mop has a tendency to smooth the metal and round off sharp edges. If for any reason the piece becomes caught up on the mops, just let go. Your work may be completely damaged, but this is better than hurting yourself. Use Tripoli polishing compound first on the metal and then rouge, working from a calico mop through to a soft wool mop for a high polish. The mops should be kept separated from the two compounds. After you have reached your desired finish wash the piece in hot water with washing-up liquid.

It is advisable to polish chains by hand, but if you need to machine polish it is important that you are very careful as chains are susceptible to becoming caught up around the spindle. To polish a chain safely, fix it onto a flat length of wood around the back with masking tape. Make sure the chain is attached really tightly so it will not fly off as you press it up against the mop.

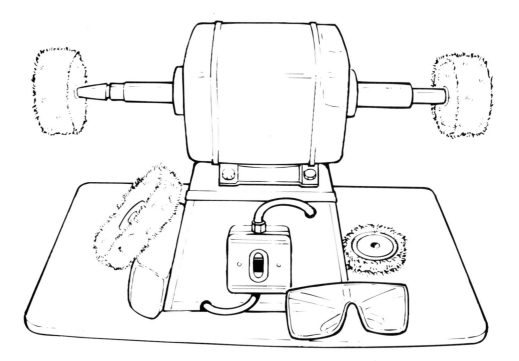

■ Polishing motor, mops, polishing compound and safety glasses.

Inlaying

Inlaying one piece of metal into another piece of metal of a different colour can create a wonderful effect and there are many ways this can be done. It is usual for the inlay metal to be flush to the surface, although it is possible for the metal to be relief. The appeal of inlaying one metal into another is the contrasting colours.

Japanese Inro purses are full of beautiful inlay work which is extremely delicate. In this case, the inlaying metal has been held in grooves or channels that have been chiselled into the base plate. Once the inlaid metal has been positioned in the grooves there should be enough surrounding metal to be pushed over with a burnisher, like setting a stone. This work is so exquisite that I recommend you visit your local museum or look in the local library or bookshop to see for yourself.

Inlaying tools

Chisel

This is a sharp-ended piece of forged, hardened steel. It has two parts: a striking end called the shaft and a cutting section, which is the blade. Chisels are used for many different jobs, including bevelling, carving, cutting, engraving and shaping metal. There is no need to attach a wooden handle to the tang of this tool because the chisel is used with a hammer to cut the grooves. When hit with the hammer the chisel should penetrate the metal surface, lifting it away. The different chisels used for various jobs include:

- Flat and chipping chisels for general purpose use and chipping and cutting into the sheet.
- Diamond-shaped chisels for square corners.
- V-shaped chisels for creating grooves to inlay, such as wire.
- Half-round chisels for creating curved grooves and holes.

Chasing hammer

This hammer has one flat and one ball-shaped end. The end you use for striking the chisel is the flat end. It is a light hammer with a springy handle.

Pitch

The pitch will support the metal and keep it in place as you work. Used also in repoussé, hard pitch holds the piece securely so you are able to chisel into the metal without it moving. For instructions on using pitch refer to repoussé and chasing in Chapter 7.

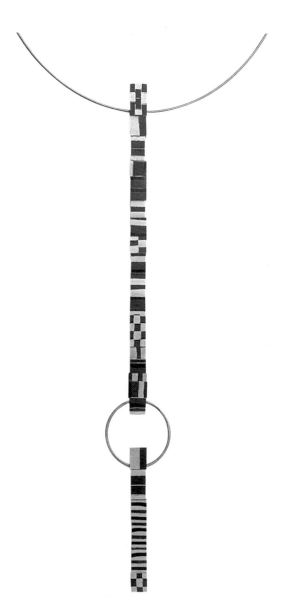

■ Inlaid necklace – mixed metals.

Inlaying copper wire into silver sheet

To make dots

You will need: a basic tool kit; wire and sheet metal of different colours

1 Drill holes the size of the desired spots into a sheet of metal.

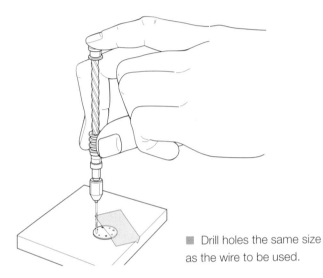

■ Drill holes the same size as the wire to be used.

2 Use wire of the same diameter as the drill bit. File one end of the wire and cut to the width of the metal sheet.
3 Borax the holes and place in the wires.

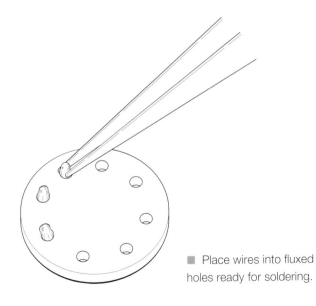

■ Place wires into fluxed holes ready for soldering.

4 Place very small pieces of solder around the edge of each hole, touching the wire.
5 Solder the wires in place and clean in the pickle.
6 File the wires flush with the metal surface.

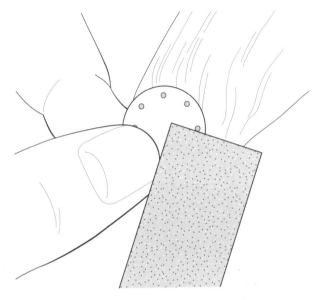

■ Once soldered, file wires flush with metal surface.

To make stripes

You will need: a basic tool kit; bowl of pitch; paraffin; chisel; sheet and wire metal of different colours.

1 Using a black marker or jeweller's scribe, mark onto the silver sheet the areas where the copper wire will be inlaid. As this is probably your first attempt, try to keep your design simple.
2 Place the silver sheet into a bowl of pitch (see repoussé and chasing section in Chapter 7) and let it cool and harden.
3 Chisel the grooves for the wire.
4 Remove the metal from the pitch and clean in white spirit.
5 On a steel block, hammer the lengths of wire into the grooves until you have a snug fit.
6 Place borax in the grooves with the wire and small pieces of silver solder around the edge.
7 Solder the wires in place, pickle and clean the whole piece.
8 File away any excess solder and overlapping wire, until the surface is smooth.
9 If any gaps appear, just fill with more solder.

Inlaying sheet into sheet

You will need: a basic tool kit; two different coloured metals.

Inlaying one shape into another shape requires a perfect fit. To ensure this the cut-out area should be used as a template for the inlaying piece.

1 Decide on your two metals, and on one sheet of metal draw the area which is going be saw pierced. The inlay piece should be a different colour and can also be patterned or textured in some way, for example roll-printed or etched.

2 Cut this shape out, remembering to drill a small hole on the inside of the drawn line to fit the saw blade through.

3 Draw round the cut-out shape (template) onto your inlaying metal. This metal should be the same thickness, or slightly thicker if you want a raised surface. Stick some double-sided tape onto the template to keep it secure while you are drawing.

4 Saw round the inlaying metal following the outside edge of the drawn line, allowing for the width of the saw blade.

5 The cut-out shape should now fit into the other piece of metal.

6 Flux around the edges with borax on the front and the back. Turn the piece over and place small bits of solder around the join. Solder the two pieces together. The reason for soldering at the back is to stop any solder running over the front, especially if the piece is patterned.

7 Not only do you now have contrasting colours but you could also have contrasting finishes, for example satin and polished, or one area oxidized.

■ Right: mixed media brooch. Some objects are held in compartments behind clear plastic riveted in place.

9

Riveting

Riveting is a method of joining materials together without the use of heat. It involves fitting a wire or tube through a tight hole and then splaying the ends until the components are held securely together. The rivets that hold the pieces in place can be completely invisible or have different shaped heads and this can become an intrinsic part of the design.

Because no heat is involved, riveting is a useful method for joining materials which cannot be subjected to heat or soldered, such as plastics and certain metals. Rivets can be bought with rounded heads. To use these rivets a hammer and two special tools are required. They resemble punches with domed depressions the size and shape of the rivet head in one end.

Riveting

You will need: a basic tool kit; vice; riveting punches; rivets.

1   Measure the thickness of the rivet using a micrometer and choose an identically sized drill bit.
2   Hold the pieces to be joined securely together by hand or using tape. Drill through them.
3   Place one of the tools in a vice with the dish shape pointing up.
4   The rivet is put through the hole and the head is rested on the tool in the vice.
5   The shank should be cut down and filed flat and perpendicular so that only 1 mm is protruding.
6   The other tool is placed over the protruding end and hammered until the wire has been shaped into another domed head and the pieces are fixed securely.

You can make your own rivets for use with the same tools. Instead of buying a rivet which already has a head, the end of a wire can be heated until it forms a ball. This is riveted in exactly the same way, the ball turning into a dome when it is hammered on the punch.

To make an invisible rivet the hole must be countersunk. Use a slightly larger drill bit than the hole size to taper the hole. A rivet of exactly the same metal must be used. Once riveted the head is hammered out to fill the countersunk area. It can then be filed so it is completely flush, and finished with the same surface as the rest of the piece.

Tube riveting

In tube riveting the wire is replaced with a section of annealed tube.

Tube riveting

You will need: a basic tool kit; centre or doming punches; tube.

1   Drill a hole the same diameter as the outside diameter of the tube so that the tube fits snugly.

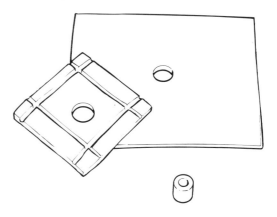

■   Drill holes the same diameter as the tube.

2   Place a domed punch, slightly larger than the tube, or a centre punch in a vice. The tube is rested on the punch and another round-ended punch or centre punch is hammered onto the other end of the tube.

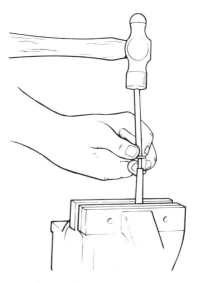

■   Using punches and a hammer, the tube splayed to make a rivet.

3 Turn the piece and hammer the other side. The ball end of a hammer can be used to finish flattening off the rivet. The resulting rivet will have a hole through it.

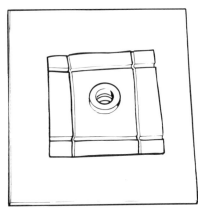

■ The two pieces riveted together.

A tube can be soldered onto any head but you will need a support that does not damage the head while you hammer over the tube rivet. A variation is to saw down the centre of the tube, so that when it is hammered the tube will open out into two separate petal like shapes.

If a very decorative delicate head is to be used on a rivet, methods involving too much pressure are not practical. Bend a wire in half and solder it onto the back of the head. Push the wires through the hole and prise them apart, flattening them like a paper clip. Do not exert too much pressure on the front of the work.

If there is to be more than one rivet in a piece, care has to be taken to ensure that all the holes line up on both sheets. Drill all the holes through the top sheet with only one hole going right through to the bottom sheet. Rivet this hole securely and then drill the other holes right through and rivet.

Riveting is also used as a mechanism to allow movement, and two pieces can pivot on a rivet if there is a slight gap. A gap can be made between two riveted parts by riveting cardboard or thick paper between them. This can be burnt or soaked out once the rivet has been made. For a wider gap or to prevent two parts rubbing, a length of tube can be slipped over the rivet between the two parts to be joined.

Riveting is an awkward business and it is sometimes handy to have an extra pair of hands.

10

Catches, hinges and findings

The way that jewellery is attached to the body or to clothing is very important. It has to be secure and easy to take on and off but as well as being practical, it is always more appealing if catches and pins have been designed with the rest of the piece in mind.

Brooch pins

A joint, a pin and a catch are the elements used to attach a brooch to clothing. The joint and catch are soldered to the back of the brooch. The pin is attached to a joint which allows it to swivel up and down. The catch holds the pin shut when it is attached to clothing.

Sometimes it is not possible to solder the joint and catch onto a brooch, perhaps because the material cannot withstand heat. In these cases more consideration must be given to decide on the most appropriate method of attachment. Gluing or riveting may be a solution, but it is advisable to first solder the joint and catch onto a larger metal back plate. This gives the glue more surface to grip and makes it less awkward to rivet. Steel and titanium cannot be soldered but they are strong enough to be used as a pin. If time is taken at the design stage, parts of the brooch can be cut and bent, without removing any metal, to make a pin and catch.

A simple brooch pin

You will need: a basic tool kit; tube; sheet metal; wire for pin.

1 Take a piece of tube with an inside diameter the same thickness as the pin wire and cut it to approximately 1 cm in length, depending on the size of the brooch. A good thickness for the pin wire is 0.8 mm.
2 File down the two ends of the tube to make them straight and smooth. A joint tool is useful for cutting the tube straight.
3 On the back of the brooch solder the tube at the right hand side. If it is a long vertically worn brooch, then it should be soldered horizontally at the top. Take into consideration how the piece will hang. If it is a large, heavy brooch it may need two pins, one at the bottom and one at the top.
4 Make a catch to secure the pin. First cut a small round metal disc using a disc cutter or a piercing saw and file the edges smooth.
5 Drill a hole in the centre of the disc, the same diameter as the wire that is going to be used for the catch. Solder approximately 1 cm of wire into the hole using hard solder. Clean in the pickle.

6 Bend over the wire to make a hook using round-nosed pliers. Trim if necessary and file the end of the wire until smooth.

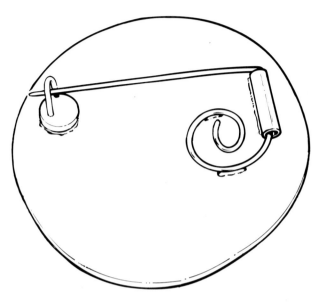

■ Completed hook.

■ Solder on hook and joint tube and attach pin.

7 Using easy solder the catch is soldered on the opposite side to the tube. Make sure the hook is positioned so the pin clips in from the underside and the pin can run from the joint to the catch in a straight line.

8 One end of the pin wire secures the pin in the joint and gives the pin spring, this can be shaped to complement the piece. If using steel wire heat the end to soften it. The wire may be flattened with a hammer and then bent at right angles, or it can be curved and slightly hammered to add interest.

9 Put the pin through the tube, pulling it tight against the already shaped end. Using pliers to hold the pin near the tube, bend the pin round until it fits into the catch. If the pin does not have enough spring to safely hook into the catch, hold the wire either side of the tube with flat-nosed pliers and twist slightly in opposite directions.

10 Cut the pin wire to the right length, just after the hook. Taper the end using a coarse file, then emery it smooth so it can pass through material easily. Filing steel will wear down the file very quickly, so if possible use an old file.

Steel works well as a pin because it keeps its shape and is very springy. It cannot be soldered directly onto the metal but must be fixed on using a joint. Springy wire alloys are also produced now. These are called spring alloy wire, or pin wire, and are available in silver and gold. The gold remains springy even after soldering, but when the silver pin wire is heated it loses its springiness.

Catches

Bar catch

This is a catch used to join a necklace or bracelet. A large jump ring is attached to one end of the necklace and a bar to the other end. The bar slots through the large hoop, holding the necklace together.

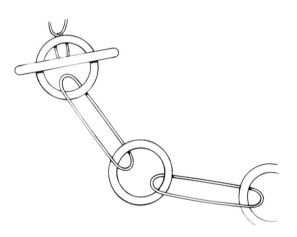

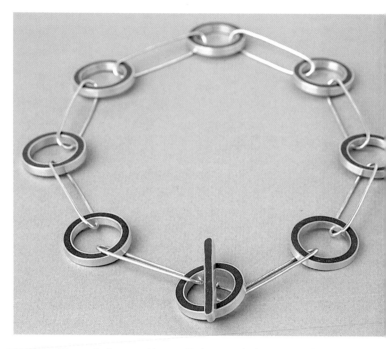

■ This slate and silver necklace with bar catch demonstrates how a catch can be an important aspect of a design.

■ Bar catch.

'S' catch

This is a catch made from wire bent into an 's' shape. It can be as large or small as you like, but the thicker the wire, the larger the catch. The wire ends can be beaded to give it a more finished appearance. To bead the wire hold one end in reverse-action tweezers. Paint some flux on the end to be beaded, then hold the torch flame just above the wire end until the metal runs into a ball. Remove the heat when you have achieved the size of ball required, then bead the other wire end. The catch is made by curving the wire into an 's' shape with ring pliers or round-nosed pliers. Solder one side closed to form a loop and slightly open up the other side to form a catch. Lightly hammer the catch to harden it. The 's' catch can be attached to one end of a necklace with a jump ring through the loop. To attach the two ends simply link the catch through a jump ring on the other end of the necklace.

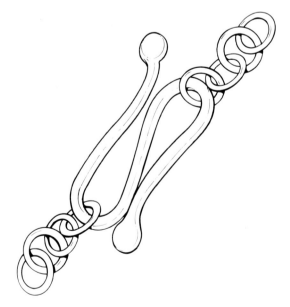

■ 'S' catch.

The paper necklace by Emma Gale in the colour photograph has a magnetic catch. The catch was designed to resemble other units within the necklace. Because of the delicate nature of the necklace the catch had to be easy to use without touching any of the paper sections. The catch works by pulling the magnets apart.

Hinges

Hinges are a useful way of joining and introducing movement into a piece. A hinge may be used on a locket or to make part of a piece flip or bend. The components of a necklace or bracelet may be hinged so that it can be wrapped around the contour of a neck or wrist.

Making a simple hinge

You will need: a basic tool kit; tube; wire.

1   File a 45° angle along the two edges of metal to be joined with the hinge. Lay the two sheets of metal flat with the filed edges touching so that it makes a triangular channel.
2   Round off the channel using a round needle file, until it matches the shape of the tube. You will find it easier to use a non-tapering round file but a tapered one is also fine.

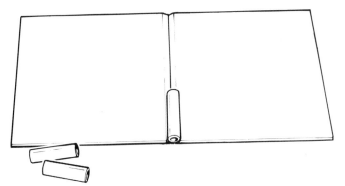

■ Two separate sheets of metal with filed edges and tubes.

3   Measure the length of the hinge and decide how many tubes will be required; there should always be an odd number. The tubes are called knuckles. A small piece of work will only need three knuckles, but if it is larger use more to prevent the hinge becoming weak and wobbly. If the amount of metal on one side of the hinge is more than on the other, use a greater number of knuckles on that side.

■ Paper, Perspex and silver necklace with magnetic catch.

4 Cut the tube into three pieces. If possible use a joint tool to ensure that they are cut straight. File the edges to clean off any burrs.

5 Make sure the areas to be soldered are clean and free from grease. Paint borax only on the places you want to solder. Hopefully this will prevent the solder running right along one side, making the hinge useless.

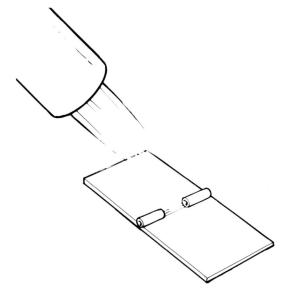

■ Soldering first two knuckles.

6 Carefully position small pieces of solder so that they are in contact with the metal and the tube. The centre tube should not be fluxed or soldered yet. It is used as a spacer and can be painted with rouge to prevent solder running along it.

7 Solder the two end knuckles, removing the heat immediately when the solder melts. Remove the inside knuckle and complete the soldering so that it runs right along the two knuckles.

8 The two soldered knuckles can be painted with rouge and the hinge then re-assembled. The middle knuckle should be soldered to the other sheet with the same care as taken before.

9 Clean in the pickle. The two pieces of metal should still come apart. All other work on the piece must be completed before the hinge is finally joined.

10 To assemble the hinge, push a snug fitting wire through all three tubes. Cut the ends of the wire leaving a small amount protruding from each end. Stand the hinge on its end so that one wire end rests on a steel block or riveting tool and tap the other protruding wire with the ball end of a hammer until it spreads. If the hammer is too big use a punch or riveting tool. Turn the piece over and hammer the other end until the wire is secure. This wire resembles a long rivet; see Chapter 9 for some ideas on different heads that can be used.

■ Join the hinge together by riveting in a wire, using riveting tools and a hammer.

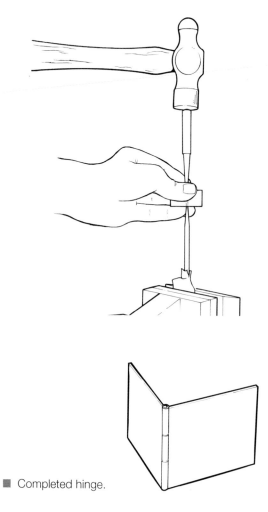

■ Completed hinge.

Findings

rivets

discs

chains

gimp to wrap over thread

nylon thread for beads

jump rings

beads

chain ends

pendant cup

earring clips and screws

earring scrolls

earring posts

bead and ring for earrings

hook wires and hoop for dangly earrings

earring flat plate and post

trigger clasps for necklaces and bracelets

bolt rings for necklaces and bracelets

swivel catch for necklaces and bracelets

barrel clasp for necklaces

cufflink fittings and chain

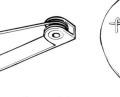
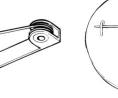

brooch revolver safety catch and joint

brooch back

stud back with pin

Earring wires

If earring wires are soldered onto metal it will become soft. The wires must be burnished to make them hard and strong again. On a steel block use a burnisher or the side of a scribe to rub the wire, turning it so that the whole wire is burnished. Use 0.8-mm silver, gold or platinum wire to make your own ear wires. Stainless steel wire is also fine to go through the ear when making dangly earrings. Ear backs can be bought at findings suppliers.

11

Stone setting

Stones of all colours and sizes have always been a very popular aspect of jewellery. Initially stones were simply tied or strung onto a string but the techniques of cutting, polishing and setting stones have developed into very skilled jobs. It is unusual for a jeweller to cut their own stones; they are cut by specialists and bought from stone dealers. Although many jewellers set stones there are craftspeople who specialize in the technique and jewellers often turn to them if they are using a particularly precious stone, such as diamonds, or if they are attempting a difficult setting.

Stone cuts

A stone may be cut in several ways. Factors that affect the choice of cut are the opacity (opaqueness), translucency or transparency of a stone. Transparent stones are cut to allow light to enter and refract, but a more simple cut is sufficient for opaque stones.

The simplest preparation of a stone for jewellery is a whole or slice of stone that has been highly polished. Crystals in their natural state are also occasionally used. Pebbles can be polished easily using a barrel polisher. The barrel imitates the action of rocks rubbing together in rivers or seas but the finish has a far higher polish than occurs in nature. Although these are the simplest cut of stones they are not necessarily the easiest to set because their shape is often irregular. A different approach to setting may be required for each individual stone.

Probably the most common type of stone cut and the easiest to set is called a cabochon. Most opaque stones are cut in this way. A cabochon stone has a flat base and is available in a variety of different shapes. The shape refers to the shape of the base, the cut of the cabochon stone is domed and smooth. Some stones, such as cat's eye stones and star stones, contain unusual tricks of the light, which are most effective in a cabochon cut. You may be most familiar with the common round and oval cabochons.

Transparent stones with good refractive qualities are cut with many facets. These faceted stones come in a variety of different cuts. The type and shape of the cut are chosen to utilize as much of the raw material as possible. These type of cuts enhance the brilliance of a stone and intensify any colour within it.

■ Right: silver, synthetic faceted sapphire and spinal rings in box settings.

Stone settings

To introduce a stone into a piece of jewellery it must be held in place without the use of heat. This is achieved using a setting. The piece of jewellery must be completed with the setting soldered in place before the stone is fitted and excess metal is pushed over. There are a variety of different settings used for different situations. The type of stone usually dictates the setting chosen. Stones differ in hardness, so a soft stone like an opal needs more protection than the hardest of all stones – the diamond. Faceted stones gain extra sparkle if light is allowed to catch them from different angles. The setting chosen may also be a purely aesthetic decision that complements the design of the piece of jewellery.

One of the easiest settings to make yourself is a rub-over setting or bezel setting. This setting can be used on cabochon and faceted stones. Claw settings are normally used on faceted stones because the majority of the setting is open allowing the maximum amount of light into the stone. A huge variety of claw settings can be bought from a findings supplier. You can also make your own, although it is a fiddly job that must be done accurately.

Bezel setting

A bezel or rub-over setting involves making a tight-fitting metal wall (the bezel) around the stone. The stone rests on a wire or ledge inside the bezel or on the sheet of metal the bezel is soldered to. When the stone is fitted into the bezel the very top of the wall is pushed against the slope of the stone to hold it in place. Bezel strips of fine gold and silver can be bought from metal suppliers. You can also use metal from your own stock if it is cut into strips and is thin enough to push over the stone.

Box bezel setting

A box bezel is a rub-over setting where the stone rests on a metal back plate and the surrounding metal is cut away. The stone is the dominant feature. The setting allows you to attach findings to make a pendant, brooch or, if you have two similar stones, a pair of earrings.

■ These rings show different shapes of stones and unusual ways of setting them. Linda Miller shaped the blue lapis lazuli herself from a solid block.

Making a box bezel setting

You will need: a basic tool kit; bezel strip or thin strip of sheet metal; setting tool; (optional) triblet and hand burnisher.

1 Take some bezel strip, no wider than the height of the stone. The length of bezel required can be calculated using two equations.

Round stone bezel =
diameter of stone $\times$ π + thickness of metal.

Oval stone bezel =
2 x length + width + thickness of metal.

Another way of making the bezel fit is to wrap it around the stone and mark and cut where the strip overlaps.

2 Cut and file the ends of the strip and shape it around the stone to check that it fits.

3 If the bezel appears to fit the stone bend the two ends together. At this stage the shape of the bezel does not matter as long as the two ends are aligned with no gaps. Secure it in place with binding wire.

4 Solder the join using a small amount of hard solder. The solder is usually harder than the metal used for the bezel, so if too much solder is used it will be difficult to bend with the rest of the setting.

5 Once the setting has been soldered it is shaped to fit the stone. To shape the setting for a round stone a triblet can be used. A triblet is a steel tool with a round section tapering to almost a point. Small ones that are ideal for making stone settings are available. The soldered bezel is fitted onto the triblet and tapped with a mallet to make it round. Slide it off and put it back on the other way to counteract the taper on the triblet. Because you are working on a small scale it is probably not necessary to secure the triblet in a vice. Hold it in one hand and rest the end on the bench. If you do not want to invest in a triblet, round-nosed pliers are perfectly adequate, while ring pliers may be useful for oval settings.

6 The shaped setting should now fit the stone snugly. Remember you will not be able to push the stone in curved side first once the back is soldered on so make sure you can still fit the stone in by dropping it in base first. If the stone does not fit well it is worth taking time at

this stage to try again. If the setting is too large cut down the solder line. A saw blade may remove enough metal to make it fit, if not file the ends before re-soldering. If the setting is too small it can be stretched slightly on a triblet by hitting it with a mallet while pushing it further up the triblet.

7 Now that the setting fits, the top and bottom are rubbed flat using some emery paper on a flat surface. At this stage the height can be checked. The bezel needs to be slightly higher than the curve of the stone. Lay the stone and bezel on a flat surface next to each other to judge the right height, rubbing away extra metal if necessary. If you prefer the bezel can be left higher, allowing a thicker band of setting to be pushed over.

8 Check that the setting is still the right shape for the stone and then solder it with medium solder onto a sheet of metal. Steel clips can be used to hold the setting in place while soldering but check that pushing the clips on has not altered the shape.

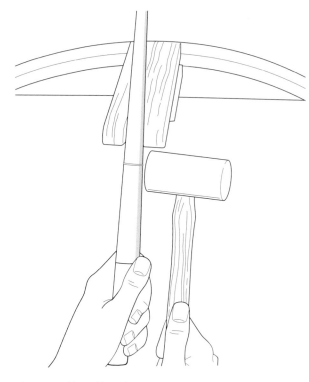

■ Shape soldered bezel on a round triblet with a mallet.

9 Once the setting is soldered and cleaned in the pickle the excess metal from around the edges can be cut away. Saw as close to the solder join as possible but try not to touch the setting. File it and emery to make the edges smooth. If you want to test the stone at this stage, melt some beeswax on the end of a pencil or small piece of dowling. This can be placed on top of the stone to allow you to lift it in and out.

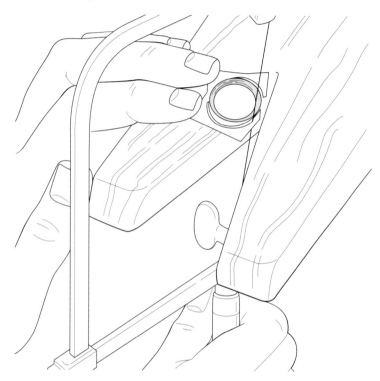

■ Solder shaped bezel onto a back plate and saw out using a piercing saw.

10 Solder on your chosen fittings – these may be for a brooch pin or some jump rings so that a chain can be threaded through. Protect the other solder joins with powdered rouge to prevent them running.

11 Pickle and finish the piece ready for the stone to be fitted (see Chapter 8).

12 It is important to gain a good grip on the piece when setting. A ring may be held in a ring clamp or a brooch rested on a block of wood that allows the fittings to hang over the edge.

13 Using the stone setting tool the metal is pushed over onto the stone. Working around the stone pushing the bezel over results in a build up of metal. To avoid this, small sections at a time are set. Push one part down and then move across and set the same point on the opposite side, then set in between these points. This continues until all the metal has been pushed over. Now you can work your way around the setting checking all the metal has been set equally and smoothly.

■ After all soldering and filing is complete, set the stone using a stone setting tool.

14 If necessary carefully file away any marks with a safety back needle or escapement file. A burnisher rubbed around the setting will smooth and polish it.

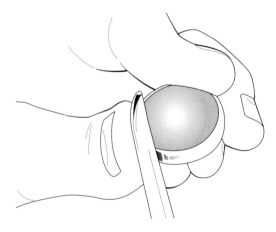

■ Burnish the setting until smooth and polished.

To make a square box setting, the bezel strip should be measured, scored and bent to shape (see Chapter 7). Once the initial shape has been made excess metal from the corners must be removed. In the corners saw a small line to locate a triangular needle file. At a slight angle file away some metal from each corner. Enough metal should be removed so that when the setting is pushed over the corners meet but do not overlap or leave a gap.

A ledge bezel setting

In a ledge bezel setting the stone rests on a ledge rather than the back plate. This setting allows a stone to be set up high or have an open base to let light in. Ledge bezel can be bought and fancy patterned designs are available but it is easy to make your own.

Making a ledge bezel setting

You will need: a basic tool kit; bezel strip or thin strip of sheet metal; setting tool.

1 Make a bezel to fit the stone snugly as if you were making a box bezel.
2 Using narrower bezel strip construct another bezel so that it fits tightly inside the first. This makes the ledge to rest the stone on.
3 The bezels are pushed inside each other so that the base rims are flush. The top of the outside bezel should be higher than the inside bezel, allowing metal to be pushed over the stone to complete the setting.
4 If this setting has a back plate there is no need to solder the inside bezel in place.

A tube setting is another version of a ledge setting. It is a useful way of setting small round-faceted stones. A tube with an outside diameter larger than the stone and an inside diameter smaller than the stone is used. For this technique you need a pendant drill and a setting burr. The setting burr should match the diameter of the stone as closely as possible. The burr is used to carve out a ledge in the centre of the tube. If the fit is good the stone should snap into place and the excess metal can then be pushed over.

■ The slate in this necklace has fine silver on the inside edge.

Setting faceted stones

Although faceted stones can be set using a bezel setting, there are more traditional settings. A crown or prong setting enhances the brilliance and colour of a stone by allowing light in from various angles. Pavé setting is a method of covering an area in small stones, usually of a similar shape and size. Small stones are a lot less expensive than rarer large stones, and set closely together in this way they can be very effective. Small parts of the surrounding sheet metal are engraved into notches to hold the stones in place. Gypsy settings also use the surrounding metal to set the stone flush into the piece. If you wish to master some of these technical settings there are many specialist books on the subject.

Open settings can be made incorporating a bezel like the ones already discussed. The prongs are cut into the setting, then bent back. The stone is then put in place and the tips of the prongs are pushed back over to secure the stone. A variation on this method involves soldering prongs around the outer edge of the bezel. If the bezel is tapered, the prongs do not have to be bent back.

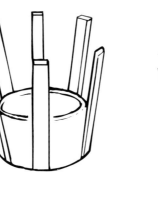

■ Prong settings.

Tapered setting

A collet plate is a steel block with variously sized tapered holes. An annealed tube is placed in a tapered hole that allows it to drop halfway in. The punch is positioned in the tube and hammered, making the tube take on the tapered shape of the hole. Although a collet plate and punch are useful there is another method of making a tapered setting that does not involve any specialised equipment.

Making a tapered setting

You will need: a basic tool kit; pair of compasses; paper; calculator.

1 Measure the diameter of the stone and transfer this measurement as a line onto paper, adding a little extra to allow for the thickness of the metal.
2 Draw a side view of the collet you are making, using the line already drawn as the top line.
3 Extend the two lines that represent the sides of the collet down until they meet. This is the centre point where the compass will be positioned to make the arc for the cone.
4 Position the compass on the point and draw an arc round from the top left hand corner and then another arc from the bottom left hand corner.

 diagram of collet

template

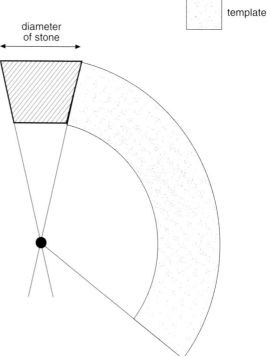

diameter of stone

■ Template for making a tapered bezel.

5 Measure the diameter of the stone and multiply it by π to calculate the circumference of the stone and add on a little extra to compensate for the metal thickness. Mark out this measurement on the outer arc and from this point extend a line down to the centre point.

6 The template is now completed for the tapered setting. It can be cut out and stuck onto the sheet of metal.

7 Saw out and clean up the edges with a file and emery paper.

8 Shape it with round-nosed pliers so the two edges meet to make a cone.

9 Solder the two edges together using a little hard solder.

10 The shape of the cone can be trued on a scribe or small triblet.

11 Place the stone in to check that it fits and remove any extra metal from the top and bottom. Emery the bottom (the more tapered end) so that it is flat and the setting can stand level.

Crown setting

A crown setting is a more complicated version of a prong setting. It can look very professional when made well. It is made up of a cone shape that is then filed and cut to make the claws and open work. The metal must be relatively strong because the design is so delicate. Gold or platinum are almost always used for these types of setting.

In this chapter the subject of stones and incorporating them in jewellery has only been touched upon. There is much to be learned about stones, their properties and their exciting possibilities in jewellery making. Stone suppliers are listed at the back of the book. You will be surprised at the selection of different types, colours and sizes available. Even stones such as sapphires and rubies can be bought relatively cheaply, and although they may not be of superior quality they are still appealing. See the photographs of Anna Gordon's rings.

■ These rings are of precious metals set with aquamarine, peridot and amethyst. The stones are all bezel set.

12

Enamelling

Enamelling is the technique of fusing coloured glass to metal using heat. It is an excellent method of introducing colour and pattern into metalwork. Traditional enamelling requires some skilled metalworking techniques, but similar results can be achieved using simpler methods. It can be great fun experimenting with the most basic techniques, such as scratching patterns into dry enamel before firing. See Ann Little's enamelling in the photographs.

The transformation of the pale dry powder before firing to the bright glassy colours when removed from the kiln minutes later is captivating. Enamelling can be very spontaneous and exciting at the final stages of applying and firing, but allow time for preparation if you wish to avoid problems and predict results.

Safety
- *When using dry enamel powder wear a dust mask as the small particles are harmful to breathe in.*
- *The kiln and anything removed from it are very hot. Wear gloves long enough to cover any exposed skin when working with the kiln, or use a very long firing fork.*
- *Always wash hands after using enamels.*

You will need: a basic tool kit, kiln, enamels, glass brush, lollipop stick, material mesh and elastic band, firing fork, firing tray, carborundum stone.

■ Left: silver, slate, resin and enamel brooch.

■ Right: the patterns in this enamel necklace were created by drawing in powder and layering colours.

Equipment and materials

The kiln

The most important piece of equipment when enamelling is the kiln. Kilns vary enormously in size, price and type. There are two main types of kiln, gas and electric.

A gas kiln uses bottled propane or natural gas and tends to heat up faster than an electric kiln. An electric kiln plugs into a household socket, and is often smaller and cheaper than a gas kiln. You could compare it to the difference between cooking on a gas and an electric stove. The size of your work should determine the size of the kiln you buy, but don't restrict yourself by choosing something too small.

Pyrometers and regulators are extras which can be bought. A pyrometer is a temperature gauge and may be advisable if you want to fire enamels accurately. It is possible to gauge the temperature of a kiln by the colour inside. A red/orange colour indicates the ideal firing temperature and with practice you will soon become aware of subtle colour changes within the kiln. A regulator controls the temperature of a kiln. It will click on and off to maintain a certain temperature and allows you to turn the heat up or down. If you have no regulator, when the kiln glows a bright yellow/orange (too hot) simply open the kiln door or switch the kiln off until it reaches its optimum colour/temperature again.

Without a kiln

It is possible to do small items of enamelling using a jeweller's torch instead of a kiln. The flame of the torch should not touch the enamel so a structure has to be built to support the work and allow the flame to be played underneath the piece. This could be a metal tripod with a wire mesh platform.

Enamels

Enamels are available in a huge variety of transparent, opaque or opalescent colours. Transparent enamels allow light to pass through. The colour of the transparent enamel varies depending on the metal or colour underneath it. If the surface underneath the enamel is bright, the colour will appear more brilliant. Transparent enamels are often used on silver or gold because of their reflective quality. Different depths of transparent enamel create different intensities of colour, and they therefore work well over engraving or any technique that introduces different depths and textures into the metal. Opaque enamels allow no light to pass through, and will conceal any metal or enamel underneath. If some opaque enamels are overfired they become translucent but revert back to opaque when fired again at a lower temperature. Opalescent enamels have a milky translucent quality and require very accurate firing to work successfully.

Different enamels have different optimum firing temperatures. These temperatures should be supplied with the enamels when you buy them. There are hard, medium and soft enamels. Hard enamels melt at a very high temperature, medium at a medium temperature and soft at a low temperature. Soft enamels are usually applied last when enamelling as they can burn out at higher temperatures. Clear fluxes are used as a base or final glaze.

Enamels are available in lump or powder form. Powdered enamel is easier to use as it has already been ground by the supplier. Lump enamel involves a lot of hard work with a pestle and mortar to reach the powdered form required for enamelling. To remove any impurities the powdered enamel should be washed, and this is especially true for transparent enamel.

Metals

Copper is an ideal metal for beginners to enamel on because it is cheap and easy to work with. It has a melting point of 1083°C which is much higher than the melting point of enamels, making it hard to spoil your work by melting the metal in the kiln. Silver and gold are also used in enamelling. Special enamelling quality silver is available, but although it contains fewer impurities than ordinary sterling silver this still does not solve the problem of fire stain which can cause dark patches to appear under the enamel. Fine silver does not have fire stain but it is extremely soft, making it impractical for use in some pieces.

Not all metals are suitable for enamelling on. Do not enamel on brass, gilding metal or bronze because they contain a percentage of zinc. Zinc has a very low melting temperature, causing it to bubble in the kiln. Cast metal contains many impurities, making it unsuitable for enamelling.

■ Silver, paper and enamel layered brooches. When the enamel is rubbed back with a carborundrum stone, the roll-printed writing is revealed.

Preparation

Many of the problems which arise in enamelling can be prevented if care is taken at the preparation stage.

Metal

All the soldering and metalwork involved in making a piece of enamel work must be completed before enamelling begins. You may wish to enamel simple shapes which can then be set like a stone. This avoids the problem of solder joins which can weaken if put in a hot kiln repeatedly. Special enamelling solder has a very high melting point but it does not run along joins as readily as ordinary solder. It should be stick soldered and not cut into small pieces. To stick solder, paint one end of the enamel stick with flux and hold the other end with reverse-action tweezers. Heat up the piece to be soldered and when it glows a dull red push the end of the enamel into the join. The solder should melt on contact with the metal and flow into the join. If you find enamelling solder difficult to work with hard solder will probably be sufficient for your needs.

Cleaning metal in preparation for enamelling

1 Metal must be very clean to allow the enamel to fuse with it. First anneal the metal, as this will get rid of impurities and grease on the surface and soften the metal.
2 Once annealed the metal is pickled and then rinsed in water.
3 Scrub with a glass brush (these can be purchased from any enamelling stockist) on the surface of the metal using water. Watch out for little bits of the glass brush that come off, as they can get in your fingertips and hurt. If you don't have a glass brush, rub with wet and dry paper and then scrub the metal with a brass brush and some washing-up liquid.
4 The metal is grease-free when water covers the surface in a sheet and does not pull away from areas, causing big droplets.
5 Dry with a clean cloth. Only clean the surface that is to be enamelled on. Be careful not to touch the surface once it is cleaned as fingers may leave grease marks.

Enamels

Enamels contain many impurities so it is best to wash them. To wash powdered enamels place the quantity required in a screw-top glass jar. Cover the enamel with water, filling the jar about half full. Screw on the lid and shake. Allow the enamel to settle on the bottom. The water will appear cloudy. Pour the water off and repeat the process until the water remains clear after shaking. The final rinse should be done using distilled water.

The enamel should be completely dry before it is placed in the kiln. If it is wet the water will boil in the kiln, making the enamel splatter. If you plan to wet-pack the enamel leave just enough water in the jar to cover it and pour this into a palette or small dish. If you wish to apply the enamel dry place it in a clean flat dish and cover with a clean cloth. To dry quickly place on the top of the warm kiln, stirring the enamel to get rid of any lumps. The clean enamel should be kept in jars with tight fitting lids somewhere dry, as moisture can make enamels deteriorate. Remember to label the enamels well with manufacturer's name, code, colour and firing temperature.

Applying enamels

The first coat of enamel is very important. It should be thick enough to generously cover the surface of the metal. If it is too thin the enamel will burn away in places revealing the black copper underneath. This firescale cannot be removed easily using pickle because it contains some enamel. If transparent enamel is applied too thickly and unevenly, cloudy patches appear and a texture like orange peel covers the surface. These can continue to show up after subsequent firings. Opaque enamels benefit from a slightly thicker first coat than transparent enamels. If you require a very rich, deep colour it is better to apply several thinner layers rather than a very thick one.

The coat of enamel must be even. The same problems of burn away and orange peel can occur if it is uneven. Be careful not to allow build up in the centre of the piece; it is better to have thicker enamel around the edges where it can become too thin and burn away.

Counter enamelling

Problems may arise when enamel is fired onto only one side of the metal. Metal and enamel cool and contract at different rates, creating tensions that cause the metal to buckle and dome. Sometimes the enamel will crack and ping off. This problem can be solved by firing enamel onto the back of the work first. If the enamel is applied to both sides of the piece the tensions balance out, preventing movement in the metal. This is called counter enamelling.

Counter enamel can be made up of any enamel but often consists of leftover and contaminated enamel. This works well because mixed enamels have different melting points, which prevents the counter enamel slumping when hot. A good counter enamel is 50 per cent hard flux and 50 per cent mixed colours.

■ Silver brooch with roll printing and enamel.

Counter enamel is dusted on dry. The thickness of the counter enamel should be a similar thickness to the enamel on the other side. It can be applied thickly as it will undergo many firings, making the surface gradually smooth out and defects disappear. Once the counter enamel has been applied and work begins on the other side remember that every time the piece is returned to the kiln the counter enamel will melt again. This means that the work must be carefully supported to prevent the counter enamel melting and sticking to the stand, leaving messy marks. Make your support before you start enamelling. As little as possible of the support should touch the counter enamel.

If you think counter enamelling is too difficult to apply to your design, there are other solutions. It is advisable to counter enamel square, rectangular or pointed shapes because enamel breaks off the corners easily but rounded and domed shapes cause fewer problems. Metal naturally domes in the kiln, so if you dome it before firing less movement will be likely to occur. Also, if the copper you use is over 1 mm thick counter enamel is not required.

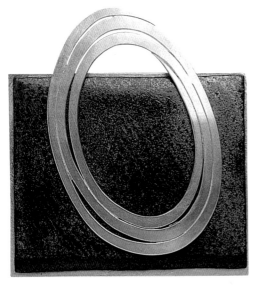

■ Silver and enamel brooch. The enamel is layered with many colours. Patterns are created by scratching into the enamel before it is fired.

Dry application of enamel

The simplest method of covering large areas with enamel is to dust on dry enamel. Wear a dust mask for this as tiny particles float up and they are not healthy to breathe in.

Dusting on enamel

1 A clean piece of paper should be laid down in your work area. This will catch any spare enamel which can then be poured back into the jar after use.

2 Place your work on a lollipop stick or something similar. Once the metal is covered with enamel the lollipop stick makes it easier to lift it by the edges onto a firing tray.

3 The enamel is sieved onto the metal. A sieve can be bought but it is easy to make one. A fine tea strainer may be sufficient or fine fabric mesh can be stretched over a small jar of enamel and fixed with an elastic band.

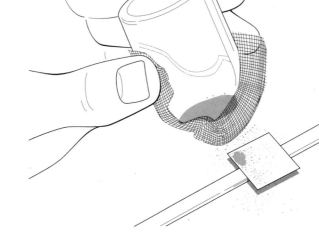

■ Dusting on powdered enamel. A sheet of paper catches excess loose powder.

4 If your work is not flat it should be painted with gum available from enamel stockists to help the enamel stick. The gum is painted on using a sable paintbrush. It dries fast so you must work quickly.

5   Start sprinkling the enamel onto the edges and then work into the centre keeping the coat even.

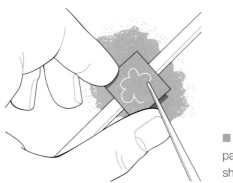

■ Scratching on a pattern with a sharp-ended tool.

6   Lift the enamelled piece onto a firing tray and leave for a few minutes to allow the gum to dry properly.

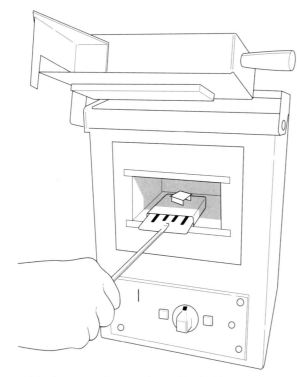

■ Placing enamel-covered metal in the kiln.

7   Fold the paper with the spare enamel in it and pour it back into the jar. If it has been contaminated with the wrong colour use for counter enamel.

Wet application of enamel

More control over applying enamel can be achieved using wet enamel. Wet inlaying is used in traditional techniques, such as cloisonné, champlevé and plique-à-jour, where care has to be taken placing different colours of enamels into cells created in the metal. The wet enamel is applied gradually in small quantities, but although the enamel is applied wet it must be completely dry before firing.

Three tools are required for wet application of enamel: a spatula; a poker; a spreader. They can be bought but are also easy to make.

Making tools for wet application of enamel

You will need: a basic tool kit; wine-bottle cork; copper wire or the metal from a paper clip.

1   To make the spoon-shaped spatula, hammer the end of one wire flat and file the flat edge round.

2   The poker is straight and pointed so file the end of the second wire to a point.

3   To make the spreader bend the third piece of wire at right angles.

4   Attach a handle by poking the end of each tool into its own cork.

■ Wet application tools.

Wet application of enamel

You will need: enamelling equipment, spatula, poker and spreader.

1 The enamel that has been previously washed and placed in a palette is dragged out with the spatula. The spatula should contain mostly enamel and not be waterlogged.
2 Place the enamel onto the surface to be filled, using the poker to scrape off the enamel from the spatula and work it into the corners. Apply small amounts of enamel until the area is covered in an even thin layer.
3 Use the spreader to spread the enamel evenly and tap the side of the piece to flatten out the wet enamel. If there is too much water, hold some absorbent paper against the edge of the wet enamel to draw the excess water off.
4 Allow the enamel to dry completely before it is fired, placing it somewhere warm like on top of the kiln.
5 You may find it difficult to lay wet enamel next to dry enamel because the dry enamel will suck the water away. Dampen the whole piece with water spray or brush a little water where you want to wet pack before you start.

Firing

Firing is the most exciting part of enamelling. After all the preparation this is when you see the enamels come alive. At this stage you can work very intuitively and spontaneously, layering lots of different colours together.

The piece should be placed on a support for firing. The support should be made of stainless steel as this will not produce firescale which can ping off and ruin a piece of enamelling. It should touch as little of the piece as possible so as not to mark the counter enamel. This support is then placed on a stainless steel stand. A mesh stand works well because the holes allow the heat to circulate around the whole piece. It is shaped so that a firing fork or spatula can be slid underneath to lift it up.

The kiln should be preheated. Different kilns take different lengths of time to heat up. Some should be left an extra half hour after reaching the desired temperature to allow the heat to penetrate the bricks. This prevents too much loss of heat when the door is opened. The manufacturer will supply instructions with the kiln when you buy it.

Enamels are fired between 750°C and 900°C (1400°F and 1650°F). There are several factors that affect the length of time required for the firing. The hardness of the enamel, the size of the item to be enamelled and the time taken for the stand to heat all affect the firing time. Firing can take from one minute to several minutes. It is necessary to keep checking progress during the firing.

Before you place the stand and enamel in the kiln check that the piece is dry and free from dirt as these can cause pitting in the enamel. If there are specks of dirt they can be removed using the wet tip of a paintbrush, taking care not to disturb the enamel. The kiln is very hot so take great care when opening and closing the door. Use a very long-handled fork or spatula which is heat resistant and can fit under the mesh tray to pick it up. We use a barbecuing spatula which has a long handle on it.

Wearing protective gloves, slide the fork under the tray and open the kiln door with the other hand. Lift the tray in, placing it steadily in the kiln. It may take practice to be able to do this without shaking and disturbing the enamel. When you have the hang of it you should be able to place your work in the kiln very swiftly. The aim is not to leave the door open too long, allowing heat to escape. Once your piece is in the kiln you should keep an eye on the progress of the enamel, either through the peephole or by opening the door slightly. During firing the enamel darkens, then appears to go bumpy and finally turns completely smooth. The smooth surface is usually avoided until the final firing. Using the fork remove the piece from the kiln when the enamel has gone darker and glassy but not completely flat. Place it on a heat-resistant brick and allow it to cool down. Do not plunge it in water or try to cool it too quickly as this can cause the enamel to crack. Initially the enamels will appear dark, and it is interesting to watch as the metal slowly cools down and the colours appear. The oranges and reds appear last so do not worry if they are not visible when first out of the kiln.

If you cannot achieve a smooth, even surface and there are holes and bubbles, this could be due to several factors:

- The metal may not be pure enough. If a metal contains too much of the wrong metal enamel will not bond with it.
- The enamels may not be clean enough.
- The enamel could be damp or too thinly spread.
- The piece may have been underfired for too short a time or at too low a temperature.

When all enamelling is completed the piece can finally be pickled and polished. These procedures affect some enamels so it is wise to experiment on test pieces to avoid ruining the completed piece. Fire the enamels you have used onto small squares of metal and try pickling and polishing them. It will become clear if the enamel reacts badly to the treatment.

Traditional techniques

Enamelling techniques traditionally used in historical jewellery and metalworking are still used by jewellers today. They require the enameller to be accomplished in skilled metalworking techniques, such as engraving. There are easier ways of achieving such effects and you can experiment with different tools and methods. The techniques all have French names and all involve the wet application of enamels.

Champlevé

This method involves carving out recesses in the metal that are then filled with layers of enamel until they are flush with the top of the metal. The traditional method of creating these cells is engraving. Engraving can be used to create very intricate, clean patterns and is an ideal method to use in champlevé, but it requires great skill.

A similar effect can be achieved by etching. Etching involves masking out the metal with special varnish and then drawing into the areas to be etched. It is easier for those with less experience in metalworking to draw fluidly and achieve their desired results with this technique. Etching is not the perfect method to use because when acid bites into metal it eats sideways as well as down, creating an undercut, and the etched lines can be quite ragged. The technique is explained in full detail in Chapter 8.

Another method of producing champlevé is to saw shapes out of one sheet of metal and solder it to another sheet twice the thickness, creating recesses. With this technique care has to be taken to remove any traces of solder in places where enamel is to be laid. Solder can go black and make the enamel cloudy.

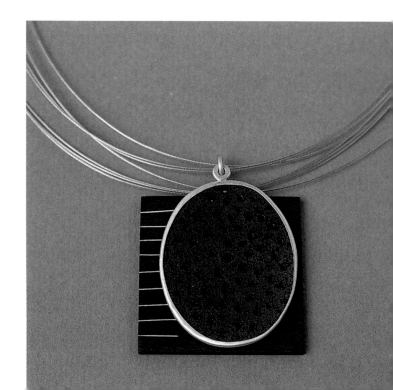

- Silver necklace featuring slate and enamel. A deliberately thin layer of enamel is used on copper to produce black speckles and black edges around the holes.

Cloisonné

Cloisonné is another method of creating cells to pack wet enamel in, but the cells are made using wires. Special cloisonné wires can be ordered from enamel suppliers. Round wires may be used but when the final piece is rubbed down the wires will look thicker than expected. If you wish to make your own wire use 0.3 mm round wire and slightly flatten it with a hammer. The wires then have to be shaped to create your pattern. Use round-nosed pliers or bend the wire round a pen with your fingers. Traditionally, wires were soldered to the metal base but this can cause problems for beginners as messy solder has to be carefully cleaned up in order not to spoil the enamel. If you intend to solder, use hard or enamelling solder. An easier method for fixing your wire design to the base is to fire a layer of transparent flux over the metal first. Once the layer of flux has been fired onto the metal allow it to cool. Lay the cleaned, shaped wires onto the flux; they should stand easily if the wire has been shaped. This is then re-fired until the wires sink into the flux. If overfired the flux will creep up the sides of the wire and when the coloured enamel is added this will make the edges appear bleached. Once the wires have been fixed the wet enamels are packed into the cells as described earlier in wet packing and built up in layers until they have reached the top of the wires. The piece can now be stoned down using a carborundum stone (available from enamel suppliers) with water and rubbed with wet and dry emery papers for a very smooth effect.

Baisse-taille

Baisse-taille relies on transparent enamels and the metals underneath for its effect. This technique involves texturing metal which can then be seen through transparent enamel. The deeper the pattern, the more intense the colour appears. One colour of transparent enamel can appear darker or lighter depending on the pattern underneath. Engraving, etching, using a burr on a pendant drill, or hammering and punching can create interesting patterns and textures. Engraving and burring also make the metal more reflective which works well under transparent enamel.

Plique-à-jour

Plique-à-jour creates an effect much like stained glass. There is no metal backing so light can shine through the transparent enamels in the cells. Plique-à-jour can be made by piercing shapes out of sheet or constructing cells using wire. This technique involves quite a lot of skill and patience because the enamel has to stay in cells without a back plate. This is easier if the holes you are trying to fill are no bigger than 1 cm and they are rounded shapes with no sharp corners. Use reasonably thick metal, remembering that when it is finished it will be rubbed down on both sides. A sheet of mica to lay the piece on can be bought from enamel outlets. Pin the metal to the mica using pins of stainless steel. Fill the holes with wet enamel, trying to drag it across so the water and enamel hold in place. Place in the kiln, not allowing the piece to get too hot or the enamel will creep away from the sides. Remove from the kiln when it has just begun to melt and still appears granulated and fill any gaps until it reaches the top. Then stone down both sides and give it a quick hot flash firing.

For larger pieces of plique-à-jour, the techniques of cloisonné and champlevé are used and then the backing is carefully etched away.

Creating simple effects

Breaking the rules

Enamelling is a great technique for playing with and much can be learnt by simply having a go. You may find you want to approach it in a very spontaneous way. Although all the techniques for avoiding problems have been explained, try experimenting and breaking the rules – you may like the results. Don't give up on a piece of enamelling if you don't like it. Rub some of it back with a carborundum stone or put a layer of enamel on top to change the colour. Overfire it so colours become more transparent or metallic and to see how the enamel burns away in patches. Try playing a very soft flame over the enamel to see if it changes the colours.

Playing with powder

Simple but effective results can be achieved by scratching away powdered enamel. Once fired these lines can be filled with another colour which will be revealed when rubbed back with a stone. Stencils can be made by cutting shapes out of card, placing them on enamelled metal and dusting on another colour and then removing the stencil to reveal the pattern. Gum can also be used to paint patterns on a base coat of enamel. The enamel dusted on will stick to the gum and the rest of the enamel can be shaken off, like using glitter. Try embedding wires into the enamel. Special foils can be bought that create a lovely bright surface under enamels.

■ Brooch of mixed metals with enamel. A lead pencil can be used to draw onto enamel that has first been matted with a carborundrum stone. Firing in the kiln should fix the pencil marks.

13

Casting

Casting is the process of pouring molten metal into a mould. The mould is made using a master or by carving out a shape directly into a soft heat-resistant substance. The metal solidifies in the shape of the mould. This technique can be used for the mass production of identical items or for one-off pieces, depending on the method of casting used.

Casting is an ancient process, but the basic techniques first developed are still used by craftspeople today because they are simple and involve little equipment. Some of the first copper axes were cast by pouring molten copper into soft stone carved with the shape of an axe head. The techniques of charcoal block casting and cuttlefish casting are primitive methods still used by some jewellers. Another early method of casting involved making a model in wax or resin which was then coated in clay. A hole was left in the clay so that when fired the wax seeped out leaving a mould to be filled with molten metal. This technique has evolved and been developed to a high standard so that good quality identical items can be mass produced with predictability. The equipment is expensive so jewellers often make a master that is then sent to specialist companies who have had many years of experience in casting.

■ These silver cast figures form an attractive brooch.

Charcoal block casting

Simple castings can be made using soldering blocks of natural willow charcoal. Charcoal is particularly suitable for use in casting because it reduces the amount of oxygen absorbed by the molten metal. The shape to be cast and the crucible from which the molten metal will be poured are both carved into one block of charcoal. The mould can only be used once and the casting will be flat on one side.

Charcoal block casting

You will need: a basic tool kit; two charcoal blocks; scalpel or engravers.

1 Select two blocks of charcoal large enough for the design and the crucible to be carved from.
2 In one block of charcoal carve a design. Charcoal is soft so a scalpel or engraver will cut it easily. The depth of the carving equals the thickness of the casting. It is a common mistake to make castings too thick and heavy but it is also important not to make the mould too shallow. This would prevent the metal filling the mould completely and would result in castings that are too weak. Press some Blu-Tack into the carving to take an impression of the design and see what the finished casting will look like.
3 Carve a hollow 2 cm from your design that is large enough to hold the amount of metal you require.
4 Join the two carvings by cutting out a canal for the molten metal to flow from the crucible to the mould.
5 Take the other charcoal block and place it flat over the mould leaving the crucible and part of the canal exposed.
6 Tie the two blocks securely together using binding wire.
7 Estimate the amount of metal needed to fill the mould and part of the canal – it is better to overestimate than underestimate. If too little metal is used it can cause problems such as porosity, giving a pitted, sometimes crumbly surface.
8 Place the metal in the crucible and heat it with a strong flame until it melts into a moving ball.
9 Using tweezers or a metal prod tip the blocks so that the metal flows into the mould. Keep the blocks at an angle for a minute until the metal has cooled.
10 Untie the blocks and remove the casting with tweezers, leaving it to cool completely. The extra metal from the canal is then cut off and the casting is cleaned up.

■ Silver and gold rings with cast elements.

Cuttlefish casting

Cuttlefish casting uses the bone from a cuttlefish. These can be bought in pet shops. It is a suitable substance for casting because it is soft enough to carve but it is also heat-resistant. Three-dimensional castings can be made using this method but the mould can only be used successfully once.

Cuttlefish casting

You will need: a basic tool kit; a cuttlefish bone; crucible; long-handled tongs.

1. Choose a decent sized cuttlefish bone which is not too crumbly.
2. Using a fine blade saw off the top and bottom of the bone which tend to be fragile.
3. Saw the cuttlefish in half along its length. The depth of the cuttlefish bone determines how deep your casting can be. The cuttlefish bone has a natural grain running through it which will be translated onto the casting.
4. Rub the two halves flat on fine wet and dry paper placed on a flat surface such as a sheet of glass or steel block. The two halves should fit together perfectly with no gaps. If you find it difficult to cut the cuttlefish bone in half, use two bones of a similar size and rub each flat on a sheet of wet and dry.
5. This technique works particularly well if a model is used. The model can be an existing object or made out of a material that will withstand the pressure of being pushed into the cuttlefish: plastic or wood are appropriate. There must be no undercuts in the model. Alternatively, carve a design into the cuttlefish bone using a scalpel or engravers.
6. Taking one half of the cuttlefish, press the model in until it is almost half the way in. The thickest part of the model should be nearer the base of the cuttlefish, furthest from where the metal will flow in. The only force used to propel the metal in this method of casting is gravity. Your design should not involve the metal flowing back up the way.

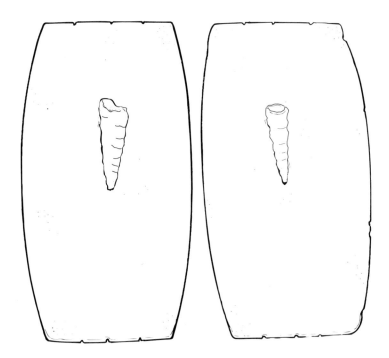

■ The cuttlefish is cut in half and sanded flat with a seashell pushed in.

7. To ensure that you can realign the mould once the model has been removed make pins out of copper wire or matchsticks; three pins should be sufficient. Push them into the cuttlefish bone, not too close to the model or the edge of the bone, and don't go right through the bone.
8. Take the other half of the cuttlefish bone and align it with the half containing the model. If you hold them between your knees you can use knee pressure as well as the force of your hands to ease the two parts together. Push gently and firmly until the two halves meet.
9. If the two halves do not align perfectly when they are pushed together, shape them with a file and smooth both ends flat. Score lines using a saw or file on the sides of the cuttlefish where the two halves meet. If these line up when the mould is finally assembled you can be sure that the mould is perfectly aligned inside.
10. Gently prise the two halves apart.

11 Keeping the model in place to protect the mould use a knife to score several lines radiating out from the impression in the mould but not reaching the outside of the cuttlefish bone. These are vents to allow the gases produced while casting to escape.

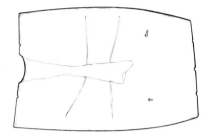

■ Impression of object with channel cut for metal to flow down. Scored lines let gases escape and pins locate the two halves.

12 A tunnel to pour the metal into the mould must also be made. Cut a cone shape, making it wider at the point where the metal will be poured in and thinner where it meets the impression of the mould.

13 Remove the model carefully and brush away any dust. If the brush is used too forcefully, the texture of the cuttlefish bone will become more evident. This may be used to your advantage if you want a textured surface.

14 Fit the mould back together, making the pins and lines match up. Tie it securely with binding wire.

15 Stand the mould on its end with the carved hollow facing up. Use fireproof bricks for support or press it into a fireproof container filled with damp sand. Remember to stand it on a fireproof surface such as a heat-resistant soldering mat.

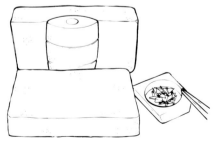

■ Two halves of the cuttlefish bound together with binding wire, supported with fireproof bricks. Ceramic crucible with silver off-cuts and powdered flux.

16 If a model has been used to make the mould, the amount of metal required for casting can be estimated by filling a transparent beaker with water. The model is dropped into the water and the water level is marked. The model is then removed and metal is added in small lumps until the water reaches the line again. Extra metal should be added to ensure a good casting.

17 Place the metal with some borax in a crucible. A ceramic crucible can be bought or one can be carved out of a charcoal block. Powdered borax works well; scrape some off your borax cone and sprinkle it over the metal to be melted.

18 Melt the metal using a strong torch flame. When the metal has melted into a moving molten ball, pour it into the mould.

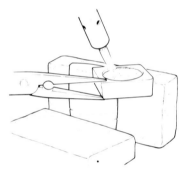

■ Metal heated in crucible, held with long metal tongs and ready to pour into the cuttlefish.

19 Allow the mould to cool for 10–15 minutes before pulling the two sections apart.

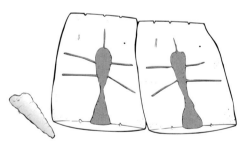

■ Cuttlefish opened after casting. Cast object is now ready to be filed and cleaned up.

20 Remove the casting with tweezers and allow to cool.

21 Excess metal should be sawn off and the casting cleaned up.

Lost wax casting

In the lost wax process models are made using wax. Wax is available in sheets, blocks and wires of different hardness. Dentistry wax is sometimes used. It is easy to sculpt using engravers or a scalpel. The scalpel can be warmed to smooth the wax and to melt sections that are to be joined together.

The model is fixed to a base with a sprue and button of wax. The sprue makes the tube down which the metal will flow. A metal tube or flask is placed over the model and secured with melted wax to the base. The mould is made using a special plaster called investment that can withstand high temperatures. The investment is mixed with water and poured into the flask. Air bubbles can spoil a casting. To make these rise to the surface the mixture is placed in a vacuum or tapped on the bench. Once the investment has set the base is knocked off and the mould is placed in a kiln to burn out the wax. While still hot from the kiln molten metal is poured into the mould. A centrifugal machine is used for this process because it forces the metal into the mould, making incomplete castings less common.

The lost wax process relies on the model being burnt away, leaving its impression behind in the plaster. Wax is not the only material that serves this purpose and some natural objects can also be effective. Objects such as leaves and seed pods work well. They can be made more robust by spraying with hairspray. If an object is very thin and delicate it may not cast. A thin leaf can be coated with wax on one side to strengthen it but the fine texture of the leaf will only be evident on one side of the casting. The burning out of a natural object takes slightly longer and creates more fumes than burning out a wax model.

If many castings of the same item are required a master is made in metal, this is used to produce a rubber mould. By injecting wax into the rubber mould lots of identical wax models can be made. If these are sprued like a tree a number can be made in one casting.

Most jewellers working from a small workshop do not have equipment for lost wax casting. They make a metal model and send it to a specialist company who will produce a rubber mould and send back the number of castings requested. It is a skilled job to produce good quality castings.

■ The textures on these cast brooches were first made in wax, then cast into metal.

14

Plastics and resins

Plastics are often considered to be a modern material, but natural plastics have been used to make jewellery for centuries. Naturally occurring plastics include amber, tortoiseshell and ivory. Recently tortoiseshell and ivory have been reproduced using synthetic plastics as this is a cheaper and more humane alternative.

The word plastic is derived from the Greek *plastikos* which means 'to shape or mould'. Synthetic plastic jewellery may be considered cheap and tacky and have a throwaway image, but pieces of jewellery made from the first synthetic plastics are now collectors' items. Exquisite one-off pieces can be created taking full advantage of plastic's qualities.

Plastic is the perfect material for producing large, striking and colourful jewellery because it is lightweight and durable. There are two types of synthetic plastics. Thermoplastics can be softened by heat and reshaped. Thermosetting plastics set extremely hard when a catalyst is added. This reaction is irreversible.

■ Laminate petal brooch – mixed materials.

Plastics (thermoplastics)

Safety
- *A dust mask must be worn when sawing and filing, as the dust produced is harmful.*
- *Care must be taken not to overheat plastic.*
- *Always work in a well-ventilated room.*

You will need: a basic tool kit, wet and dry paper, dust mask, oven, kitchen foil, cotton gloves, clamps.

Plastic can be bought in sheets, rods and tubes of varying sizes and thicknesses. Different colours and opaque, translucent and transparent finishes are available.

Cutting

Plastic can be easily cut using a piercing saw or a hacksaw. A piercing saw is more effective for cutting intricate shapes. Different saw blades are used depending on the thickness of the plastic: a coarser blade should be used for thicker sheet and a finer blade for thinner sheet. Plastic often has a protective paper cover, on which the shape to be cut can be drawn. When cutting the plastic the saw may tend to stick, as friction causes the plastic to melt and jam the blade. To prevent this from happening paraffin can be poured on the section to be cut, or candle wax rubbed on the blade intermediately. Coarse-toothed blades and heavy pressure may cause chipping, and thin protruding sections could be vulnerable to snapping off.

Filing

When the shape has been cut out the edges will appear rough; these can be smoothed and shaped using a coarse hand file. A separate file should be kept for plastic work and not used on metal. If the file becomes clogged it can be cleaned using a file brush.

Carving

To achieve a more detailed form plastic can be carved. Excess material may be cut away using sharp hand tools, or for a quicker easier result a pendant drill with burrs is very useful. Carving can create an intricate surface and transparent plastic may also be carved internally so the carving can be seen through the surface. Care must be taken to watch the carving from all angles as it may look wrong from one angle. Internal carving can also be filled with coloured resin. Carving takes skill and practice but there are simpler ways to achieve interesting effects. Holes drilled part way through transparent plastic resemble bubbles when viewed from the opposite side, and these can be filled with different colours of resin. Simple textured surfaces also look good when viewed from the opposite side of transparent plastic. Experiment to see what effects you can achieve.

Sanding

Wet and dry paper produce a number of different finishes, including translucent, frosted and highly glossy. Using a small amount of water, begin sanding the piece with coarse paper and gradually work down to a fine paper. The water reduces dust and achieves a finer finish. Do not assume that for a piece to be finished it has to be highly polished. A coarse grit of paper can be used for different surface patterns. Rubbing onto the plastic in circular motions creates a swirly surface. It is this attention to detail that makes a piece of jewellery special.

Thermoforming

Plastic in a solid form can be made malleable by heating in a household oven. When heated the plastic softens and can be shaped with the hands, protected by gloves, or pushed into a mould. It must be held in shape until the plastic cools and re-hardens.

Before forming the piece should already be shaped and finished. Lay the item on some kitchen foil on a baking tray and place in a pre-heated oven at approximately 150°C (gas mark 2/300°F). In a matter of minutes the plastic will soften. Take care not to overheat the plastic as this can be very smelly and release toxic fumes. Once the plastic is softened it can be bent wearing a clean pair of cotton gloves. **If the piece is reheated it will return to its original shape**. A few attempts may be required to achieve the desired shape as the plastic cools and hardens quickly. Overworking may cause the piece to break. Another method of forming a shape is to place the plastic sheet on a basic mould; once the plastic has softened it can be pushed into the mould using an opposite die or gloved hands. A doming block and punches can be used to dome a circle of plastic. The plastic can be shaped around an object such as a jar to form a bangle. Shapes have to be kept simple to work well.

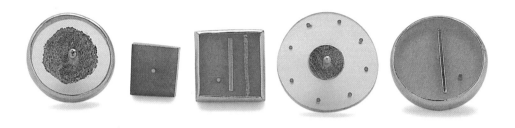

■ Earrings from Perspex, silver, gold leaf and paper.

Laminating

Laminating involves sandwiching sheets of plastic together and sealing them using heat and pressure. Great effects can be produced by placing items, such as pressed flowers, thin metal and wire and cloth, between sheets of transparent plastic. The process is similar to that of thermoforming. A hot press is ideal for this type of work, but in the home clamps and steel sheets are all that are required. Two clean grease-free sheets of plastic are placed on top of each other with the chosen object lying between them. They are put in a pre-heated oven at 150°C until soft. The room should be well ventilated for this procedure. The softened plastic sandwich is then placed on a clean, flat sheet of metal, preferably stainless steel. Another sheet of metal is then placed on top and these are clamped together tightly until the plastic has cooled and hardened. Bubbles may appear if the plastic is overheated and air bubbles may become trapped if the inclusion is too thick. Different colours of plastic can be layered using this technique although for simple layering of plastics you may find superglue is easier and faster. Multicoloured layers of plastic create interesting effects when they are carved into.

Dyeing

Safety
- *Wear rubber gloves and safety goggles.*
- *Open a window.*

Plastic can be dyed to achieve subtle and original colours and patterns that are not available in the bought range of coloured plastics. Although the dyed colours are very attractive it must be noted that the surface colour may wear off over time and fade if exposed to strong daylight.

Cleaning

The plastic must be thoroughly cleaned before it is dyed. This is achieved by immersing for 15 minutes in a 0.1 per cent aqueous solution of calsolene oil HS at 60°C. Once clean, rinse in cold water avoiding too much contact with the plastic and place immediately in the dye bath.

Dyeing process

A dye bath should be a container made of glass, stainless steel or vitreous enamelled metals. The dyestuffs used are from the 'Dylon' range and are readily available in a wide variety of colours. The dye has to be mixed with other ingredients before it is ready to use.

Formula	by volume	by weight
A Calsolene oil HS	1.85	3
B Benzyl alcohol	1.06	2
C Hot water	60	94.5
D Dyestuff	0.3	0.5

Mix A, B and D to a smooth paste and then dilute with C. The temperature of the dye bath should be at least 80°C. Place the plastic in the dye mixture for 15 minutes. For an even coverage the piece should be suspended vertically or agitated occasionally. Different intensities of colour can be achieved by varying dye concentrations or immersion time. Once the plastic is dyed, remove from the bath. Rinse immediately and dry with a soft cloth to prevent the dye from drying in patches.

Patterns can be achieved by masking off shapes before immersion in the dye mixture. The dye agent should be capable of withstanding the temperature of the dye bath and removed by white spirit or methylated spirits. Resists which you may have around the house include masking tape, araldite, UHU and Blu-Tack. Complicated patterns using different colours can be built up in layers.

Resins (thermosetting plastics)

Safety
Guidelines to the safety aspects involved when working with resins are available from all suppliers and manufacturers. It is important to follow these carefully, as incorrect use of resin can be very dangerous.

- *Eye protection in the form of goggles is very important. If the resin or catalyst comes into contact with your eyes, wash immediately with lots of cold water. It is advisable to consult a doctor. An eyewash can be purchased from a local chemist.*

- *Make sure that the room you are working in is well ventilated. Fumes given off by resins are toxic and can cause nausea and dizziness. It is a good idea to set up a small self-contained area next to a window, for which the sole purpose is resin work.*

- *As resins are toxic, it is advised that you wear a mask. Try to avoid any contact with the skin. Protective clothing and gloves or barrier cream are essential. After working with resin, wash your hands thoroughly and use a good handcream before eating or touching food.*

- *Do not work with resin near a naked flame as it is a flammable material. When setting up the self-contained area, make sure it is away from any fire hazard, such as a cooker or heater. Smoking must be completely prohibited.*

- *All rubbing down should be done wet to limit the amount of dust. This is important when sanding. Wet and dry paper is available from your local hardware store in a variety of grits. Start with a coarse paper and gradually work down to a finer grade. If you are dry filing wear a dust mask and protective goggles.*

- *Be very careful when disposing of any waste chemicals. Contact your local council and speak to the environmental safety officer, and they will advise you.*

- *Read all instructions carefully. Each manufacturer will supply you with instructions on how to mix resin. These will vary depending on the type of resin.*

Resin is an accessible, suitable and easy material to use in the home, providing these careful precautions are taken.

You will need: liquid resin, catalyst or accelerator, colour pigments, fillers, goggles, dust mask, rubber gloves, protective clothing, various grades of wet and dry paper, moulds, embedding objects, plastic cups, lollipop sticks, scales.

Thermosetting plastics are those which start in a liquid form, such as a resin, and then become solid once a catalyst is added. It is impossible once the plastic has become hard to reverse the process.

The development of plastics in liquid form has made it possible for jewellers to create in a whole new medium. Colour pastes, both opaque and translucent, can be added to the resin in its liquid state, prior to the addition of the catalyst or hardener. Such effects as shading, marbling and inlaying can be produced. Translucent resin applied onto patterned or textured metal can also create exciting effects. Resin can be used to cast into various shapes and items embedded inside.

Two main resins are polyester and epoxy. The polyester resin is a syrup-like liquid that becomes solid when a catalyst is added. It has an expiry date of about one year if stored in a cool, dark place. The catalyst needs the same attention, but will only last a fraction of the time, approximately three to four months. The epoxy resin is a clear substance. This type of resin is ideal for casting and embedding small objects, and also adding colour pigments.

Catalysts and accelerators

The hardening agent added to resin to make it set is called a catalyst. It controls the rate of hardening, reduces overheating and prevents unwanted cracking. It comes as a liquid or a paste.

A catalyst is normally sufficient to cure the resin but if a speedier result is required accelerators (activators) may be used. If you are using both an accelerator and a catalyst, there are certain procedures that must be taken into consideration:

- Work with each one separately.
- Always add the catalyst to the resin first, followed by the accelerator.
- Never mix the catalyst and accelerator together as they can react violently or even explode.
- To control the curing time vary the amount of accelerator rather than the amount of catalyst. A larger amount of accelerator reduces the curing time, while smaller amounts increase it.
- If the resin is used above room temperature (20°C) then a reduction of accelerator is necessary.

Fillers

Fillers are usually added to resin to improve colour pigments, create metallic effects, reduce shrinkage and give strength, creating a scratch-resistant surface. The filler comes in a dry powder and is then mixed with the resin before adding the catalyst. Mix everything slowly but thoroughly, ensuring that the mixture is smooth and there are no air bubbles. Metal fillers come in a dry-powdered form and include such metals as brass, aluminum, copper and bronze. These give precious metal qualities, for example red and yellow gold and silver. The combination of metal and resin gives an exciting metallic appearance. The block, once dry, can be carved, sawn, turned on a lathe and even polished. A mixture of filler to resin can be used in ratios from 30 per cent to 70 per cent or 50 per cent to 50 per cent but not more filler than resin. Metal fillers should be stored in an airtight container.

■ Nylon and Velcro form
the basis of this neckpiece.

Colour pigments

Pigment pastes can be used to colour any liquid resin. Available as either translucent or opaque in a variety of colours, they can be used to create a single coloration or mixed together to form a layered effect. As the rate of curing is slow, it is possible to build up layers of different colours. Each layer should be added as soon as the resin has become gel-like.

Mixing resin for curing

You will need: resin, plastic cup, lollipop stick, pigment paste, catalyst mould, Plasticine, petroleum jelly.

1   Measure out the desired amount of resin to the scale you require. Small plastic cups are good to mix in as they are inexpensive and can be thrown away after use.

2   Add pigment pastes if required. Always make up a little more of the coloured resin and before adding the catalyst, divide the resin into two separate pots. Only add the catalyst to one pot as the extra amount will provide you with the exact match in colour when it comes to filling in any unwanted air bubbles. When mixing in the colour paste it is likely that air bubbles will form. If this happens either let the mixture settle for a while or stand the tub in some hot water as this will encourage the air bubbles to rise to the surface and burst.

3   The next stage is to measure out the catalyst. Care must be taken when mixing and this should be done slowly and gently so no further air bubbles are produced. Mixing thoroughly is important or the resin will not set.

4   If you are also using an accelerator this is when it should be added to the resin, after the catalyst has been mixed in thoroughly.

5   Pour your mixture into a mould. The mould can be made out of plaster of Paris, wood, latex, plastic, silicon rubber, wax or clay. Plasticine needs to be secured around the base, to prevent leakage. To make the extraction of the resin from the mould easier, coat the inside with a thin layer of petroleum jelly.

6   The drying-out process can take up to 24 hours depending on the type of resin. Shallow-cast and lay-up resins dry extremely quickly once the catalyst has been added, and can take anything between 15 and 30 minutes. Even when set the resin can have a tacky surface but this can be removed using acetone, a brush or wet and dry paper. The material is now ready to saw, file, sand or turn like wood on a lathe. Resin can also be polished like metal, using a liquid metal-polisher, such as Brasso (see Chapter 8).

Catalyst or accelerator amounts added to resin weight
This is only an approximate guide; always refer to the manufacturer's guide.

Resin weight	2% catalyst or accelerator
25 g	15 drops (0.5 ml)

Embedding

Embedding objects in a translucent resin can create extremely exciting effects. A natural state of this can be seen in amber which encases complete insects. Liquid resin has enabled jewellers to encase any water-free object. These could include dried insects, dried seed pods and flowers, sticks, shells, pebbles, stamps, threads or cloth, semi-precious stones, coloured glass or plastic, or anything you can think of. It could be a way of preserving something special. If metal objects are used these may tarnish in the resin, losing their colour and shine. Hair spray can be used to strengthen a delicate object that may move or crush under the weight of the liquid resin. There are no hard and fast rules for embedding as each piece will require different amounts of resin and catalyst, depending on the scale of the object. Resin can be purchased from craft and model shops.

Moulds

Moulds can be made in a variety of media, for example an ice-cube tray, a small jelly mould, a plastic cup or the plastic tray in a chocolate box. Small plastic biscuit cutters in the shape of stars, half moons and hearts are all good shapes for jewellery. Make sure they are sealed around the base against leakage – Plasticine is good for this. Do not use any of the above items for their normal purpose once they have been used with resin. Use a flexible mould as it makes life much easier when removing the cured resin. A thin layer of petroleum jelly rubbed onto the surface of the mould creates a barrier so the resin, once dried, will come out easier.

■ These bangles are made from coloured resin.

Enamelling using resin

Enamelling onto metal is a skill that has been used in jewellery making for centuries. The application of polyester resin onto a metal surface without the use of heat has brought about a similar effect which is less expensive but just as successful.

The surface of the metal to be enamelled has to be grease-free and abrasive. Mix up the resin on a palette and apply to the metal with a brush or lollipop stick. It is possible with such small amounts to approximate the quantities of resin and catalyst as the layers being applied to the metal will be thin. It is also possible to create dimension by building up layers in different colours. If the resin is transparent, it can be interesting texturing the metal first with hammered or etched marks (see Chapter 8).

Plique-à-jour resin

This is again much simpler than true enamelling. Resin plique-à-jour involves piercing an opening into a sheet of plastic or metal, then filling with translucent resin which, when hard, allows light to pass through. To support the resin until it sets, each open section must be backed with a piece of masking tape; this is removed once the resin has dried. More resin can be added in layers to increase the amount or to create a darker colour.

See the photograph of Carla Edwards' resin bracelets.

15

The beginner's workshop

Simple jewellery can be made in a limited space using a wide range of materials and not many tools. The kitchen table can be adapted for jewellery making with a few pieces of basic equipment.

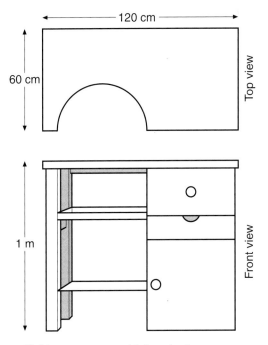

■ Here are some guidelines for the proportions of your workbench.

You will need a wooden bench peg which clamps onto the table to support the jewellery while you are working. The bench peg is wedge-shaped and has a sloping topside for resting the piece while working and a 'v' shape can be cut out of the centre for sawing. The table needs to be fairly stable, as does the bench peg, so it doesn't wobble as you work. It is important to have a close light source – an anglepoise lamp is ideal. In our workshop the benches are approximately one metre high and we all have typist chairs with a backrests which move up and down to any height. It is important to try and work at the same level as your jewellery, so adjust your seat or use a low stool with a cushion for comfort at the kitchen table. When you are soldering make sure the area is covered with a sheet of steel and on top of that the charcoal or soldering blocks. Place a tray on your lap to collect any silver or gold filings; it is amazing over the years how many jars you can fill with scrap metal which can be sent back to the bullion dealer to be re-melted. The gas supply will be in bottle form and will run from either propane or butane gas. A separate air supply is not required. The torch element with different nozzle sizes can be purchased from a specialist jewellery stockist. The bottles of gas can be purchased from gas suppliers in a variety of sizes, so a small one can fit neatly away in a cupboard. It is possible to purchase small hand-held torches which have a disposable gas cylinder.

The traditional jeweller's workbench

The traditional jeweller's workbench is made from wood approximately 5 cm thick and 1 m high. The bench needs to be firm and solid while you work. It could be made with four solid wooden legs or two legs at the front and attached to a back wall with 'L' shaped brackets. Another alternative is to build cupboard space on either side instead of legs – this way the bench is extremely sturdy and has lots of storage space. Attach a little ledge around the edge of the bench to stop bits falling down the back. In the middle there needs to be a large cut-out semi-circle; around the edge of this semi-circle a length of leather is hung to catch any filings. Some jewellers find a tray that can be attached and removed easily is more efficient. Within the centre of the semi-circle a bench peg needs to be clamped. On our workbenches we have a hook to rest the torch head and a block of wood drilled with lots of holes for small drills and files. Another good idea is to have somewhere for all your pliers and hammers even if it's just nails in the wall for them to hang on.

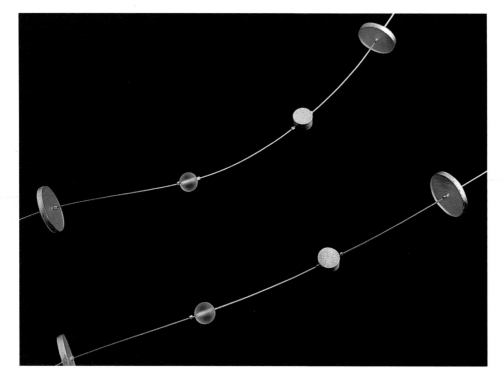

■ Above: necklace incorporating Perspex, gold leaf, silver and rock crystal beads.

■ Right: it is possible to buy ready-made workbenches, but this photograph shows a simple workbench with a section from a kitchen cupboard. Note the following: bench pegs, cut-out semi-circle, anglepoise lamp, soldering equipment, soldering blocks, tray for collecting metal filings, rolling mills, files, hammers, pliers, steel block, ring size, silver wire, scrap silver in jar, stool, plenty of inspirational material on the wall.

Glossary

π   Pi, approximately 3.14

Accelerator   Used in resin to speed up drying time.

Acetone   Used to clean off substances, for example sticky resin.

Activator   *see* Accelerator

Alloying   The combining of metals in order to change their characteristics.

Annealing   The process of heating metal to a certain temperature to relieve strains in the metal created while working.

Anvil   An iron tool used to form metal.

Baisse-taille   A traditional enamelling technique. Textured or patterned cells are covered with transparent enamel.

Base metal   A non-precious metal.

Bevelling   To cut away to a slope.

Bezel   A metal wall surrounding a stone used in stone setting.

Binding wire   Iron wire used to secure a piece of metal for soldering.

Blu-Tack   Reusable adhesive which is soft and malleable.

Borax   Flux in cone form used with ceramic dish.

Bullion   Precious metal in solid form.

Burnisher   Hand-held tool used to polish metal.

Burrs   Small, rough pieces of metal still attached after sawing or drilling or attachments to a pendant drill used for removing metal.

Butane   An inflammable gas available in bottles.

Cabochon   A domed stone cut and polished with no facets.

Calico   A cotton fabric.

Carats   The proportion of gold within an alloy of gold. The weight of a precious stone.

Carded   Fleece that has been prepared by combing with a carder.

Casting   Pouring molten metal into a mould so that it cools in the shape of the mould.

Catalyst   A hardening agent mixed with resin.

Catch   Holds a brooch pin in place or a necklace together.

Centrifugal machine   A machine used in casting which forces molten metal into the mould.

Champlevé   A traditional enamelling technique that involves filling cells with enamel.

Charcoal block   A block used to solder on in which metal can be pressed.

Chisel   A sharp-ended tool used to carve into metal.

Clamp   To hold something in place using G clamps.

Claw setting   An open setting used to set faceted stones.

Cloisonné   A traditional enamelling technique that involves creating cells to place enamel in, using wire.

Collet   *see* Bezel.

Conforming die   A die made of two parts that fit perfectly together.

Counter enamel   Enamel that is fired onto the back of a piece to prevent movement of metal when heated.

Cross section   A sliced view of an object.

Crucible   A container used to melt and pour metal.

Curing time   The drying time of resin.

Cut   The way a stone has been cut and polished.

Die   A mould used for shaping and forming metal by exerting force.

Dilute   To thin or weaken by adding water.

Draw down   To stretch, thin or shape wire using a draw plate.

Draw plate   Used to stretch, thin or shape wire.

Drill bit   Variously sized round cutting tools fixed into a drill.

Ductile   A characteristic of metal that allows it to be stretched and thinned into wire.

Embossed   A raised pattern made in metal.

Emery paper   An abrasive paper used to clean, texture and polish surfaces.

Enamelling   Melting coloured glass particles onto metal to form decoration.

Etching   Patterns made when acid eats into unprotected areas of metal.

Facet   A flat face cut into a stone.

Filigree   Delicate wire work.

Findings   Mass-produced functional elements of jewellery, including catches and earring backs.

Fire scale   The black, flaky surface which forms on copper when it is heated.

Fire stain   The grey stains that form on silver when it is heated.

Flush   Level with the surrounding surface.

Flux   Painted on areas to be soldered. Prevents oxides from forming and allows the solder to run.

Fly press   Equipment used to dome metal using a die.

Fusing   Joining two metals together by melting.

Gimp   A spiral of very fine, tightly coiled wire, with a hole through the middle like a tube, used in bead threading to protect the threads attached to the catch.

Glaze   A thin, glassy coating on the metal surface.

Grit   Rough particles on abrasive paper.

Ground   Resist used in etching.

Gypsy setting   When a stone is set flush with the surrounding metal.

Hallmark   Official stamps made in precious metal to guarantee its quality.

Hardener   *see* Catalyst.

Inclusion   A trapped object.

Inlaying   To fit one metal into the surface of another.

Investment   A special plaster, able to withstand high temperatures, used in casting.

Jig   A tool used to form and reproduce a shape.

Joint   The part of a brooch that holds the pin, allowing it to open and close.

Joint tool   A tool used for cutting tube and wire straight.

Laminate   Layered plastics, sometimes with images sandwiched in-between.

Lathe   Machinery used to carve, cut and polish cylindrical shapes, such as tube and rod.

Leaf   Thin metal foil used with a special adhesive.

Linseed oil   Available from art and craft shops. Used to soften pitch.

Lubricant   A substance that reduces friction, to make surfaces smooth and slippy.

Malleable   A characteristic of materials that allows them to be shaped and formed without splitting and breaking.

Master   The initial model from which others are produced.

MDF   Medium-density fibre board.

Mica   Heat-resistant, thin, flat sheet used in enamelling.

Mokume Gane   Layers of different metals soldered or fused together then rolled through the rolling mills. Marks are made in the surface to reveal the metal colours underneath. Often this is then rolled into a flat sheet.

Mole grips   Large gripping pliers that can be clamped shut.

Mop head   Attachment for a polishing motor available in a variety of materials.

Opalescent   A translucent glass colour.

Opaque   Impenetrable to light.

Optimum   Ideal.

Ore   A naturally occurring substance from which metal can be extracted.

Origami   The Japanese art of paper-folding using no adhesives.

Oxidize   Tarnishing on metal surface when it has been subjected to oxygen in the air or when using special chemicals.

Papier-mâché   Making forms using paper and adhesive.

Patina   A surface colour on metal caused naturally or by the addition of chemicals.

Pavé setting   Setting many stones closely together.

Perspex   Trademark name for a type of plastic.

Pickle   Weak sulphuric acid used to remove flux and oxides from heated metal, especially after soldering.

Pin vice   Tool used to hold small drill bits or wire.

Pitch Substance used to support metal when working, for example in chasing.

Plasticine Children's malleable material.

Plique-à-jour Traditional enamelling technique that resembles stained glass.

Polishing To bring up to a high shine.

Porosity Defect in some castings causing a pitted surface.

Precious metals Silver, gold and platinum.

Prong setting Holds a faceted stone in place using prongs.

Propane An inflammable gas available in bottles.

Pumice powder An abrasive cleaning powder used with water directly onto the surface.

Pyrometer A temperature gauge used in a kiln.

Refract To deflect light at a different angle.

Refractory metals Titanium, niobium.

Regulator Controls the temperature of a kiln.

Resist A substance that protects the metal surface from acid.

Riveting A method of joining that does not involve soldering.

Rivets The elements used to join pieces when riveting.

Roll-printing Creating patterns and textures on the metal surface by exerting pressure using a rolling mill.

Rouge polish Used with mechanical polishing equipment to produce a high polish.

Rouge powder Substance painted on solder seams to prevent it remelting.

Safety back file A file with only one cutting side.

Satin finish A lustrous sheen given to metal.

Saw piercing Cutting metal using a jeweller's saw.

Score To mark a line using a sharp-ended tool.

Serrated Grooved.

Setting Surrounding a stone with metal or prongs to keep it in place.

Shim Very thin sheet metal.

Shot Small steel or ceramic shapes used in a barrel polisher.

Smelting Melting down metal to extract the ore.

Soldering Joining metal using heat, flux and solder.

Soldering wig Mesh made from iron wire used for holding objects in place when soldering.

Solidify To make or become solid.

Spent Acid which no longer works efficiently.

Splaying To prise open and apart.

Sprue A rod attached to a model. When a mould is made the sprue becomes a channel, allowing the metal to flow into the mould when casting.

Stake An iron tool used to form metal.

Tallow Fats used in the making of candles and soap.

Tang The non-working end of a tool on which a handle can be attached.

Tarnish The discoloration of metal.

Tempered steel Steel brought to the correct hardness by heating and cooling.

Tensile strength The amount of working that a metal can withstand before it cracks and breaks.

Thermoforming Shaping plastic using heat.

Thermoplastics Plastics that can be softened by heat and reshaped.

Thermosetting Plastics that set extremely hard when a catalyst is added. This reaction is irreversible.

Transparent See-through.

Tripoli An abrasive polishing compound used in the first stage of polishing.

True To make exact.

Vice jaw protectors Rubber covers that are fitted over vice jaws to protect anything held in them.

Water of ayr stone An abrasive stone used with water for cleaning away fire stain and unwanted solder.

Work hardening The hardening of metal caused by stretching and shaping it. This can be reversed by annealing.

Suppliers of jewellery materials and equipment

To find local suppliers of some materials and equipment refer to the *Yellow Pages*. Here are the name and addresses of the suppliers we use.

Paper

Paperchase,
213 Tottenham Court Road,
London WC1E 7EB
Mail order tel: 020 7323 3707
Tel: 020 7580 8496
Fax: 020 7637 1225

Faulkner Fine Papers Ltd,
76 Southampton Row,
London WC1B 4AR
Tel: 020 7831 1151
Fax: 020 7430 1248

Beads

The Bead Shop,
Covent Garden,
21a Tower Street,
London WC2H 9NS
Tel: 020 7240 0931

Beadworks (mail order),
16 Redbridge Enterprise Centre,
Thompson Close,
Ilford IG1 1TY
Tel: 020 8553 3240
Fax: 020 8478 6248

Earring Things,
The Bead Merchant,
Craft Workshops,
South Pier Road,
Ellesmere Port,
South Wirral L65 4FW
Tel: 0151 356 4444
Fax: 0151 355 3377
e-mail: sales@beadmaster.com
www.beadmaster.com

Fleece

Adelaide Walker,
2 Mill Yard Workshops,
Otley Mills,
Ilkley Road,
Otley LS21 3JP
Tel: 01943 850812

George Weil with Fibrecrafts,
George Weil,
Old Portsmouth Road,
Peasmarsh,
Guildford,
Surrey GU3 1LZ
Tel: 01483 565800
Fax: 01482 565807
e-mail: sales@georgeweil.co.uk

Beads, stones and findings

Kernowcraft,
Bolingey, Perranporth,
Cornwall TR6 0DH
Tel: 01872 573888
Fax: 01872 573704
e-mail: info@kernowcraft.com
www.kernowcraft.com

Marcia Lanyon Ltd,
PO Box 370,
London W6 7ED
Tel: 020 7602 2446
Fax: 020 7602 0382

Tools and equipment

H. S. Walsh and Sons Ltd,
243 Beckenham Road,
Beckenham,
Kent BR3 4TS
Tel: 020 8778 7061
Fax: 020 8678 8669
e-mail: inmail@hswalsh.com
www.hswalsh.com

(also base metals and plastics)
Hindleys Limited,
Design and Technology Supplies,
Hillcrest Works,
230 Woodburn Road,
Sheffield S9 3LQ
Tel: 0114 278 7828
Fax: 0114 278 8558
e-mail: sales@hindleys.com
www.hindleys.com

Le Ronka,
Unit 3,
Heathfield Units,
Sandylane,
Titton,
Stourport-on-Seven,
Worcestershire DY13 9QA
Tel: 01299 873600
Fax: 01299 873601
e-mail: sales@leronka.co.uk

Sutton Tools,
37 Frederick Street,
Birmingham B1 3HN
Tel: 0121 236 7139
Fax: 0121 236 4318
e-mail: info@suttontools.co.uk
www.suttontools.co.uk

Tools, precious metals and findings

Cookson Precious Metals,
49 Hatton Garden,
London EC1N 8YS
Tel: 020 7400 6500
Fax: 020 7400 6511
www.cooksongold.com

Blundells and Sons Ltd,
199 Wardour Street,
Lonon W1V 4JN
Tel: 020 7437 4746
Fax: 020 7734 0273

Rashbel,
24-28 Hatton Wall,
London EC1N 8JH
Tel: 020 7831 5646
Fax: 020 7831 5647
e-mail: order@rashbel.com
www.rashbel.com

Findings

Ballou Findings,
15 Cochran Close,
Crownhill,
Milton Keynes MK8 0AJ
Tel: 01908 569311
Fax: 01908 260262
e-mail: order@balloufindings.co.uk

Leaf

James Laird Ltd,
18 Craig Road,
Cathcart,
Glasgow G44 3DW
Tel/Fax: 0141 637 8288

Base metals

Edwards Metals Ltd,
Unit 37A Birch Road East,
Off Wyrley Road,
Aston,
Birmingham B6 7DA
Tel: 0121 322 2366
Fax: 0121 326 9369

Steel wire and tube

K. C. Smith and Co.,
Redbrook Road,
Monmouth NP5 3NB
Tel/Fax: 01600 713227

Enamels and enamelling equipment

Milton Bridge Ceramic Colours Ltd,
Unit 9,
Trent Trading Park,
Botteslow Street,
Hanley,
Stoke-on-Trent ST1 3NA
Tel: 01782 274229
Fax: 01782 281591
e-mail: miltonbridge@mcmail.com
www.miltonbridge.mc.mail.com

W. G. Ball,
Anchor Road,
Longton,
Stoke-on-Trent ST3 1JW
Tel: 01782 312286/01782 313956
e-mail: sales@wgball.com
www.wgball.com

Vitrum Signum,
9a North Street,
Clapham Old Town,
London SW4 0HN
Tel/Fax: 020 7627 0840

Calsolene oil HS

ICI Surfactants,
PO Box 90,
Wilton Centre,
Middlesbrough,
Cleveland TS90 8JE
Tel: 01642 437476
Fax: 01642 437374

Overseas suppliers

These can be contacted through the listed periodicals
and craft council organizations.

Further reading, galleries and museums

Technical jewellery books

Textile Techniques in Metal for Jewellers, Textile Artists and Sculptors, Arline M. Fisch (Hale), 1997)

Paper Pleasures: from Basic Skills to Creative Ideas, Faith Shannon (Mitchell Beazley, 1987)

First Steps in Enamelling, Jinks McGrath (A Quintet Book, The Apple Press, 1994)

The Colouring, Bronzing and Patination of Metals, Richard Hughes and Michael Rowe (Crafts Council, 1982)

Classical Loop-in-Loop Chains and their Derivatives, Jean Reist Stark and Josephine Reist Smith (Chapman and Hall, 1997)

Gemmology, Peter G. Read (Butterworth and Heinemann Ltd, 1991)

Practical Casting – A Studio Reference, Tim McCreight (Brynmorgen Press Inc., 1981)

Setting of Gemstones, Walter Zeiss (Rühle-Diebener-Verlag, 1984)

Inspirational jewellery books

Power and Gold, Jewellery from Indonesia, Malaysia, and the Philippines Text by Susan Rodgers; Photographs by Pierre-Alain Ferrazzini (Prestel-Verlag, 1988)

Gold of Africa, Jewellery and Ornaments from Ghana, Côte d'Ivoire, Mali and Senegal Text by Timothy F. Garrard; Photographs by Pierre-Alain Ferrazzini (Prestel-Verlag, 1989)

Contemporary jewellery books

The Best in Contemporary Jewellery, David Watkins (Batsford, 1993)

The New Jewellery Trends and Traditions, Peter Dormer and Ralph Turner (Thames and Hudson, 1994)

Jewellery in Europe and America, New Times, New Thinking, Ralph Turner (Thames and Hudson, 1996)

Jewellery Moves, Amanda Game and Elizabeth Goring (NMS Publishing, 1998)

Periodicals

Crafts Magazine, Available in good newsagents and galleries; mail order from: The Craft Council, 44a Pentonville Road, London N1 9BY Tel: 020 7278 7700 Fax: 020 7837 6891 www.craftcouncil.org.uk

RJ Magazine,
Greater London House,
Hampstead Road,
London NW1 7EJ
e-mail: rj@fashion.emap.co.uk

Findings,
The Association for Contemporary
Jewellery,
PO Box 37807,
London SE23 1XJ

American periodicals

Metalsmith,
Society of North American
Goldsmiths (SNAG),
5009 Londonderry Drive,
Tampa,
Florida 33647

Ornament,
PO Box 2349,
San Marcos,
California 92079–9806
e-mail: ornament@cts.com

American Crafts,
American Crafts Council,
72 Spring Street,
New York,
NY 10012

Australian periodicals

Craft Arts International,
PO Box 363,
Neutral Bay,
Sydney,
NSW 2089
Tel: (02) 9953 8825
Fax: (02) 9953 1576

Galleries

Contemporary Applied Arts,
2 Percy Street,
London W1P 9FA
Tel: 0171 436 2344

Crafts Council Gallery Shop,
44a Pentonville Road,
London N1 9BY
Tel: 020 7806 2559

Crafts Council Shop at the
Victoria and Albert Museum,
Cromwell Road,
South Kensington,
London SW7 2RL
Tel: 020 7581 0614

Lesley Craze Gallery,
34 Clerkenwell Green,
London EC1R 0DU
Tel: 020 7608 0393

Open Eye Gallery,
75–79 Cumberland Street,
Edinburgh
Tel: 0131 558 1020

The Scottish Gallery,
16 Dundas Street,
Edinburgh
EH3 6HZ
Tel: 0131 558 1200

Electrum,
21 South Molton Street,
London W1Y 1DD
Tel: 020 7629 6325

Cath Libbert Jewellery,
The Store,
Salts Mill,
Saltaire,
Bradford BD18 3LB
Tel/Fax: 01274 599790

American galleries

Mobilia Gallery,
358 Huran Avenue,
Cambridge,
MA 02138 USA
Tel: 617 876 2109

Velvet da Vinci,
508 Hayes Street,
San Francisco,
CA 94102,
USA
Tel: +1 415 626 7478

European galleries

Alternatives,
Via D'Ascanio 19,
00186 Roma,
Italy
Tel: 066 830 8233
Fax: 068 200 2994
e-mail: info@alternatives.it
www.alternatives.it

Hipotesi
Rambla de Catalunya, 105,
08008- Barcelona,
Spain
Tel: 93 215 02 98
Fax: 93 487 06 83
e-mail: hipotesi@sct.ictnet.es

Museums

Victoria and Albert Museum,
Cromwell Road,
South Kensington,
London SW7 2RL

British Museum,
Great Russell Street,
Bloomsbury
London WC1B 3DG

Royal Museum of Scotland,
Chamber Street,
Edinburgh EH1 1JF

Cleveland Craft Centre,
57 Gilkes Street,
Middlesbrough
Cleveland
TS1 5EL

American museums

American Crafts Museum,
73 West 45th Street,
New York,
NY 10019

Cooper-Hewitt Museum,
Smithsonian Institution,
9 East 90th Street,
New York,
NY 10019

Philadephia Museum of Art,
PO Box 7646,
Philadephia 19101

Craft societies

England
Crafts Council,
44a Pentonville Road,
London,
N1 9BY
Tel: 020 7278 7700

Scotland
Scottish Arts Council,
12 Manor Place,
Edinburgh EH3 7DD
Tel: 0131 226 6051

United States
The Society of Arts and Crafts,
Contemporary American Crafts,
175 Newbury Street,
Boston,
MA 02116–2835
Tel: 617 266 1810
Fax: 617 266 5654
e-mail: societycrafts@earthlink.net
www.societyofcrafts.org

American Craft Council,
72 Spring Street,
New York
NY 10012
Tel: 212 274 06 30
Fax: 212 274 06 50

Canada
Canadian Crafts Council,
189 Laurie Avenue East,
Ottawa,
Ontario K1N 6P1
Tel: 613 235 82 00
Fax: 613 235 74 25

Africa
S.P.E.S.
7 Avenue Labourdonnais,
Quatre Bornes,
Mauritius
Indian Ocean
Tel: 230 424 74 14
Fax: 230 424 29 60

New Zealand
Creative New Zealand/Toi
Aotearoa,
Old Public Trust Building,
131–135 Lambton Quay,
PO Box 3806 Wellington
Tel: 644 473 0880
Fax: 644 471 2865

Australia
Crafts Australia,
Level 5,
414 Elizabeth Street,
Surrey Hills (nr. Sydney) 2010

Australian Council,
181 Lawson Street,
Redfern,
New South Wales

Craft Victoria,
114 Gertrude Street,
Fitzroy,
Victory 3065

Acknowledgements

We would like to thank the students and staff in the jewellery department at Edinburgh College of Art; the photographers, with special thanks to John K. McGregor and Graham Clark; the models Maxine, Hannah and Manuela; and all the talented jewellers whose work illustrates this book, all of whom are either based in Edinburgh or are graduates from Edinburgh College of Art. The support and help from our families and friends has been great.

■ Jewellers Ann Little (left) and Emma Gale at their workbench.

Photo acknowledgements

The authors and publishers would like to thank the following for kind permission to reproduce photographs:

John K. McGregor (pages 1, 5, 7, 9, 10, 13, 14, 21 *top*, 22, 24, 25, 26, 30, 32, 36, 41, 42, 43, 46, 47, 48, 51, 53, 55, 60, 63, 74, 79, 80, 81, 84, 90, 91, 95, 100, 102)
Graham Clark (pages 2, 4/5, 15, 19, 21 *bottom*, 68, 69, 73, 77, 85, 88, 96, 98, 104, 105, 110)
Molly Bullick (pages 17, 50)
Sam Sills (page 33)
Paul Gray (pages 38, 39)
Steve Godfrey (pages 56, 83)
Katy Hackney (page 92)

List of jewellers

The jewellers whose pieces feature in this book are:

Disa Allsopp (page 91)

Lindsey Bain (page 1 *top right*)
Brigitte Bezold (page 73)
Lois Brodie (pages 41, 42)
Lynne Brown (page 48)
Molly Bullick (pages 17, 36 *right*, 50)
Fiona Bullock (page 22)

Sarah Cave (page 26)

Sue Downing (page 9)
Colin Duncan (page 19)

Carla Edwards (page 102)

Julie Ann Forbes (page 10 *right*)

Emma Gale (pages 15, 18 *top*, 21 *bottom*, 53, 55, 69,
    98, 105)
Anna Gordon (pages 21 *top*, 32, 47, 79)
Jennifer Goudie (page 7)

Katy Hackney (page 92)
Claire Hillerby (pages 56, 83)
Emma Holt (page 46)

Hannah Keith (pages 33, 95)
Jennifer Kerr (page 60)

Andrew Lamb (page 1 *bottom*)
Ann Little (pages 18 *bottom*, 43, 68, 77, 80, 85, 88)

Stephanie McCleod (pages 13, 14)
Natalie McGorty (page 1 *top left*)
Linda Miller (page 74)
Grainne Morton (pages 6, 24, 63, 90, 96)

Angela O'Kelly (page 10 *left*)

Jill Paton (page 84)

Charlotte Reid (page 100)

Joanne Thompson (pages 25, 38, 39)
Claire Troughton (page 51)

Sam Vettese (pages 30, 36 *left*)

Index